PERPETUAL CITY

PERPETUAL CITY

A SHORT BIOGRAPHY OF
DELHI

÷

MALVIKA SINGH

ALEPH

ALEPH

ALEPH BOOK COMPANY
An independent publishing firm
promoted by *Rupa Publications India*

Published in 2013 by
Aleph Book Company
7/16 Ansari Road, Daryaganj
New Delhi 110002

ISBN: 978-93-82277-24-8

1 3 5 7 9 10 8 6 4 2

Typeset in Sabon Roman by SÜRYA, New Delhi

For
Amrit and Sujan
a sliver of the city they were born in

CONTENTS

CONTENTS

SECTION I

PERPETUAL CITY

PERPETUAL CITY

Of all the world's great cities washed by the tides of history, and there are only a select few of these, in which power and pomp have been concentrated for centuries, there are none which are quite like Delhi. No other city, despite repeated attempts to destroy it, or neglect it, continues to grow and reinvent itself from age to age. Capital to multiple empires, each more glorious than the one which preceded it, and now, the largest urban agglomeration in a nation awkwardly coming into its own, it looks set to reinvent itself once more—this time as a mega-city for the twenty-first century. Unfortunately, I'm not certain that the newest avatar of this city, founded in the lee of an ancient range of hills in northern India, is going to be as appealing as those that preceded it.

As a result of decades of neglect and mismanagement, of unthinking land use, and most tragically, the toxic-transformation of the holy river Jamuna (on whose banks it sprawls) to a polluted stream, the Delhi of our children's children is likely to be an unholy, abysmal mess. Pause for a moment and imagine with me if you

can, a city with the clear and languid waters of the
Jamuna meandering through her centre, much like the
Seine or the Danube or the Thames through their cities.
Imagine how such a tangible reality could have restored
the dil of the city, made her heart come alive. Yet that
was not to be. Instead, what we have is a classic urban
nightmare that has closed off everything that is good
and beautiful about this extraordinary city—its
monuments and parks, its heady aroma of flowering
trees, its abundant birds and wildlife, its incredible,
unparalleled mix of history with its unusual, syncretic
religiosity. In all my wanderings around the world,
with the exception of Rome, I have not come across as
many hidden architectural gems as there are in Dilli
and its greater capital area. Some make profound and
dramatic statements establishing their place in the sun,
others sit apart, isolated but with pride, comfortable in
their individual skins. At its most resplendent, parts of
the city merge into a single, diverse and historic cityscape
that encompasses time immemorial, through a subtle,
delicate, nuanced tapestry of cultures. But with an
astounding lack of planning, greed and incompetence,
the authorities have done their best to reduce what
could have been a wondrous city to an urban
catastrophe. Almost, but not quite, as we shall see in
the course of the book.

÷

I moved to Delhi from Bombay in the 1950s, and was
immediately struck by the broad avenues and wide

open spaces of Delhi, punctuated with weathered monuments, their aging patina reflecting the dancing rays of early morning and evening light. It was all larger than life, powerful and fragile at the same moment.

I thought then, as I do now, that Delhi was about those who rule us, and we the ruled, who are at their 'call and mercy'. It was (and is) a city of 'them' and 'us', while Bombay was, in comparison, equal and cosmopolitan, all-embracing, and did not exude that alienating sense of absolute 'power'. From Purana Qila to Red Fort and on to Rashtrapati Bhavan, the imposing walled-in 'palaces' of the emperors of yore as well as the leaders of today, the many 'Diwan-e-Khas', were, and continue to be, secluded, protected abodes, ivory towers segregated from the people at large.

The beauty and scale of the architecture of different periods stretching over thousands of years, telling the many fables of a time past, reiterating the great information technology, the phenomenal skills of the brain and hand, that has been the intrinsic strength, the real DNA, of this Indian subcontinent for aeons, boggled the mind as I began to venture into the city's extraordinary spaces, trying to navigate its infinite nuances. For me, this layered material heritage that lay scattered around my new habitat, was my first, conscious confrontation with the meaning of civilization. As I grow older, I too, have moved into another phase of exploring life, past and present, in this city, and find that I have just about scratched the surface of an incredibly complex historical reality. I have realized, over the decades, the special privilege of being able to put down my roots in a city where history becomes magical, and stories take on political and philosophical meanings. The decoding never ends in this perpetual city, which seems to have emerged full blown at some remote point in the past, and which seems to be constantly evolving into something new, a city that will forever remain an exciting, infinitely mysterious and intricate entity, yielding up its secrets slowly, always holding out, the excitement of the unknown that is just waiting to be discovered.

÷

To descend from the flights of fancy to a more prosaic perspective, Delhi actually began in the eighth century when Suraj Pal, a Tomar Rajput, established his supremacy south of the present-day city at the edge of the Aravalli range of hills. He built a temple dedicated to the sun god, Surya, and Suraj Kund (literally, 'Lake of the Sun')—a very large and dramatic circular tank, which collected and conserved the water flowing down from the hills during the monsoon. His descendant, Anang Pal, built Lalkot, the first fort of this city, remnants of which lie along the range of hills beyond the Qutab. Then, in the twelfth century, Prithviraj Chauhan inherited the twin capitals of Ajmer and Delhi from the last Tomar ruler and his grandfather—Anang Pal III—extended the Lalkot fort area and established it as Qila Rai Pithora, often described as the first citadel and capital of Dilli.

When Prithviraj Chauhan was attacked and defeated by Mohammad of Ghor, the capital was captured. Mohammad of Ghor left Qutubuddin Aibak, his slave lieutenant, in charge, establishing Muslim dominance over what had been a Rajput and Hindu period in the city's history. A sultanate took control and Dilli began to take on another socio-political and cultural avatar that would be refined over the centuries.

Iltutmish followed Qutubuddin who had begun work on the construction of a great minaret. When Qutubuddin died prematurely in a polo accident, Iltutmish completed the great landmark and christened it the Qutab Minar, a tribute to his ancestor. It is an iconic and rather spectacular minar, exquisitely carved and superbly built, that dominates the skyline of the city even today. The area around the village of Mehrauli is testimony to a fine period in architecture and style. If there is a reinvention of a part of Dilli that is happening as we speak, it is in Mehrauli where some adventurous Dilliwallahs like Momin Latif, a trained architect and serious poet, are retracing their steps to the city's early days, recreating old havelis into unimaginably comfortable and impressive homes where they live, wrapped in history, a bit removed from our hyperactive new age.

In 1290, Jalaluddin Khilji came to Dilli. His aggressive and able successor, Allauddin, established the beginnings of 'empire'. Successful military campaigns endorsed his supremacy and he soon settled down here and built the Siri Fort that encased his palace. It is said that the

1

then capital was the lively and energetic core of a flourishing 'empire' with wonderful buildings and residences. Sadly, there is nothing left of that past except for a fragment of 'wall' alongside Panchsheel Enclave in South Delhi.

Then came the Tughlak dynasty. In 1320, Ghiyasuddin began to build the fort of Tughlakabad, and four years later, he handed the reins of the empire to Mohammad bin Tughlak, his son and heir, also described as a wise fool because he decided to shift his capital from Dilli to Daulatabad in the Deccan. He failed, however, and had to return. He passed on without an heir, his baton handed to his nephew, Firozeshah Tughlak, who built the fifth capital of this city that was fast assuming the mantle of being the favoured capital of Empire. He christened it Ferozabad. His hunting lodges and jungle retreats are the only substantive remains that are left today—these dot the kikar-forested, dry deciduous lands of the Ridge of which Malcha Mahal is the most famous. Till very recently, the Mahal was inhabited by the descendants of the last Mughal emperor, who lived within the baradari, protected from intrusions by ferocious hounds.

Shahjahanabad was the last Mughal capital of India. It remains the soul of this city. The Red Fort, looking out from Lahori Darwaza to the Jama Masjid, Chandni Chowk and all the gallis and kuchhas, stood guard with the river as its protecting moat. Within its walls, the Moti Masjid, a private mosque for Shah Jahan to worship in, the Diwan-e-Khas, his private royal audience

hall, the nahar-e-behisht and the gardens, are testimony
to the scale and grandeur of Mughal architecture and
building. The ateliers were repositories of living skills
of mind and hand. The poetry and music crossed many
marked borders and carried messages of love and
longing. The poets lived in the shadow cast by the
fortifications and were nurtured and honoured by the
rulers who treasured and conserved the best outpourings
of cultural creativity. Then, during the war of
independence in 1857, the British forces overran the
city, mutilating it and leaving behind painful wounds
and indelible scars. The city crept into its shell but did
not die. It bided its time, and when the time was right,
layered over the damage caused by yet another foreign
power and carried on. But we are getting ahead of our
story. Before it would assume its rightful position as the
capital of our country, it would do duty as capital for
the British and suffer the trauma of Independence and
Partition.

In 1911, the British Government laid the foundation
stone of the imperial capital of India—the jewel in their
crown, New Delhi. The king of England had ordered
both the shift of the British capital from Calcutta to
Delhi, and the construction of an imperial capital city
in the vicinity of the last Mughal capital of Hindustan.
Endless trips were undertaken into the hinterland around
Shahjahanabad to look for an appropriate stretch of
land that could provide space for an official centre of
governance, where grand imperial buildings would be
designed and built to salute the sovereign and his
absolute power, make a statement of 'supreme rulership',

as well as have carefully planned housing and other essential infrastructure for those who ruled the colony that was India. Soon after the decision to build New Delhi was taken and the announcement made, the movement for independent India became more vociferous. But to give the British commitment to the project of building a new capital its rightful due, the Crown continued to support the endeavour. Lord Irwin was the first incumbent of the Viceroy's House, and presided over the very first beginnings of the retreat of the British Empire in India. Lord Mountbatten negotiated the unnecessary and traumatic partition of this country as the last Viceroy of India.

The trifurcation of this ancient civilization into India, West Pakistan and East Pakistan, severely injured and maimed a people and their shared legacies. It was brutal, forcing families apart, rudely tearing at the seams of a plural and resilient culture that had absorbed from all who chose to come and conquer to pattern a patchwork that was an amalgam of infinite diversity. That was the fine and enduring strength of an united India that the retreating imperial power, having lost its right to rule, demolished forever with an unthinking and rather cruel division, done carelessly from an aircraft looking down on an already raped landscape. Refugees poured into Delhi, fleeing their homes, forced to sever their firmly entrenched roots from the land they had tilled and where their forefathers had lived in peace and friendship regardless of differences of faith, having survived extraordinary hardship, they put down new roots in what was declared 'India'. Punjabi Bagh was the first colony of post partition India in New Delhi. The scars of Partition remain for those who were witness to its horror, and in the minds of their children who grew up on those destructive stories.

Metropolitan Delhi, the city of today, sits upon that last bloody layer of the last century. Building on the remains of the past, dreaming of a possible future is what makes Delhi, Delhi.

÷

The hundreds of years of history that have infused this patch of earth on the banks of the Jamuna have bequeathed to it a treasure trove of monuments and architectural wonders. Unfortunately, Dilliwallahs have become blasé about the treasures that surround them. I remember going to the Delhi Zoo for the first time in the fifties and being stunned by the backdrop of the Purana Qila, referred to as such only after the Red Fort was built, so beautiful yet rugged and powerful, with a moat encircling it, protecting it from encroachments. Emperor Humayun had his library in this qila, overlooking the Jamuna, and it was from here that he fell to his death, missing a step on the winding stairway. Some years ago the deep and mellow voice of Abida Parveen, a popular and fine Pakistani singer of sufiana, bounced off the ancient walls as she sang of love and longing with the stark ramparts as her backdrop. That was an all too rare occasion when one was able to connect with the past while living in the present.

11

malvika singh

It is disappointing to live in such an unusual city with layers of cultures, traditions and patterns of life and living, and have to contend with unimaginative municipalities and their sterile regulations and norms which deny us entry into our legacies. History should come alive and be an intrinsic part of the life of contemporary Delhi. Instead, it is fenced off, and we are forced to peer at our monuments from a distance. They remain crumbling cold edifices rather than spectacular arenas for energetic living cultures to thrive on and grow, adding value to the lives of new generations of Dilliwallahs.

OUR LIVES WERE FULL OF PEOPLE

There were always people in our home, even if my parents, Raj and Romesh Thapar, were out to dinner. Bombay in the 1950s was 'ruled' by prohibition and to have a drink you had to have a doctor's certificate declaring you an alcoholic! It read: sharabi ka naam, sharabi ka baap ka naam, and apart from being embarrassing to fill out such an absurd 'form', it was tough to get one. Nimbu paani, a sharp intellect, and the passion to be a part of creating the modern Indian state regardless of what profession you were in, were the ingredients that made up the elixir of life in those heady post-independence days. Everyone seemed drunk on freedom.

I grew up thinking that home was a place where the doors were perpetually open and a flow of fascinating people streamed in and out, talking, arguing, eating and drinking lemonade. I remember vividly, the personas of Sardar Jafri and his wife Sultana; Suds Swaminathan; the great Italian film director Roberto Rossellini; Yusuf Bhai, Dilip Kumar, who acted with my father and Meena Kumari in *Footpath*, a film by Zia Sarhady;

Semine, and Shareef Moloobhoy, an architect who had designed the furniture in our home; Bundle and Lota Sen; Mohit Sen; Mulk Raj Anand; Attia Hosain, the author of *Sunlight on a Broken Column*, and amongst the most stunning women in the world; Gerson da Cunha, Zul Vellani and Vanraj Bhatia, a delightfully mad musician; and hundreds of others, old and young, who filled our lives with ideas and excitement. Theatre and film were intrinsic to all our lives; my parents would direct and act in plays, the rehearsals of which took place in our living room, after which the 'actors' would party there through the night, often into the early hours of the morning.

Apart from the literary and journalistic crowd, the actors and directors, there were the contemporary painters, who were making their presence felt on canvas. Among them were Krishen Khanna, Akbar Padamsee, Ram Kumar, Raza, Ara, Raval, Paritosh Sen, Jehangir Sabavala, J. Swaminathan and M.F. Husain who were christened the Progressive Artists. I feel privileged today when I think of all the 'greats in the making', across virtually every discipline, all of whom were so much a part of my life when I was a young girl. I learned a great deal from them all, many of the relationships have remained, some have extended into the next generation.

My parents were lefties in those early years and edited a tabloid called *Crossroads*. One morning, it was banned by the state of Maharashtra for having said something that the authorities did not like. Cutting a long story short, my parents filed a petition in the

Madras High Court invoking a statutory fundamental right—freedom of the press. They won the case and established that Right. They were in their early and mid-twenties. Soon thereafter, the Communist Party began to use the paper as their 'mouthpiece' as such tabloids were then called; rather rapidly, for a variety of reasons, my parents got utterly disillusioned with the CPI and drifted away, depressed and ideologically debilitated. It was then that *Seminar*, their third child as my mother would refer to it all her short life, was born. The year was 1959.

Because Romesh and Raj were regarded as 'communists', there was a Central Intelligence Department man posted outside the building, 24x7, monitoring the comings and goings of a motley crew of individuals, some well known, others unknown. My grand-uncle, General P.N. Thapar, was then GOC in Poona and would drop in at the flat whenever he visited Bombay. My grandfather, who was head of the Army Medical Corps in Delhi, would come as well. Other senior officers posted in Bombay would drop by to meet them. It was believed that the CID constable watching our home reported that 'army generals' were regular visitors at this 'commie' residence, weaving imaginary conspiracy theories by such false and careless information. Whenever it poured with rain, we would go for a long drive solely in order to irritate the CID chap, as he would have to follow us on his motorcycle and get soaked to the skin. It was our innocent way of getting our own back on him for intruding on our

privacy. Politics and taking strong positions on all
issues were what we were born and brought up with,
and they became an intrinsic element of my person.

Then, one day, my grandfather retired from the army
and built a home in Delhi, settling down finally after
years of a peripatetic life. He wanted his son to be with
him. My mother was seriously distressed. Horrified by
the prospect of having to give up her free and open life
in Bombay, live with her in-laws, share a kitchen, enter
a straitjacketed existence and more, drove her to demand
an independent cottage at the rear of the house with a
separate kitchen, if only to keep the peace with her in-
laws. She had her way and we decided to move from a
cosmopolitan city to a conservative town. She was
going to leave her friends behind and she was devastated
by the prospect. Little did she know then, that over
time, her home in Delhi would be as wide open to ideas
and as all-embracing to those who came into its orbit,
as the one she was closing down in Bombay.

÷

During the years we were in Bombay, vacation time
would bring us to Delhi to visit my grandparents.
Often we would drive from Bombay, stopping for the
night in the then unspoiled cantonment town of Mhow
on the outskirts of Indore. It was a two-day journey,
travelling twelve hours a day with no stress at all on the
narrow, two-lane national 'highway' that snaked its
way through a changing topography, taking us from
the western coast inland, gently climbing and winding

16

round the ghats, clothed with mature teak trees, then descending into rich alluvial tracts of lush and fertile land, moving further north into the ravines of the Chambal, a haven for the region's dacoits, to finally enter the dry and dusty plains of northern India that surround and encompass Delhi.

On one occasion I recall flying into the capital in a Super Constellation aircraft operated by Air India. In the fifties, Delhi airport was at the edge of Safdarjung's Tomb, and it was a less than five-minute drive to 7 Safdarjung Road, my grandfather's official residence when he was still in the army. What a change from Santa Cruz and the bustle of Bombay to this calm and serene 'island' of New Delhi, seat of the government of India. Home was a Lutyens house, appointed much like all army residences with floors covered with old Persian carpets; Public Works Department furniture which in those days was generally quite beautiful and colonial looking; a formal dining room where dinners were invariably seated, not buffet like today; bedrooms tucked away off dark, cool corridors, all with large attached bathrooms that had a rear door opening on to the grounds. The bungalow was surrounded by deep verandahs where everyday activities happened—where the darzi sat to stitch our clothes, where the phulwallah allowed us to check the ripeness of the fruit we were buying, where other vendors came with their wares. It was a continuation of what life must have been like in the 'family haveli' of the distant past.

Evening entertainment was going for a drive and

ending up eating ice cream from the thelas at India Gate. Dinner was family time replete with stories and jokes, arguments and debate, all ending with a game of Dumb Charades of book and film titles. It was mandatory to read a few chapters of a book each night before falling asleep. Those delightful 'must do's' have slipped into oblivion. I would watch my grandmother dress for dinner at the Gymkhana Club across the street or at the army mess. It was a long, meticulous ritual that I would try to imitate once she had left her dressing room, only to amuse myself and feel grown-up. Before going to sleep, Dhulku, the old and grand family retainer with a turrah on his head, would tell us a bedtime story, an episode from the *Mahabharata*. It was my very first introduction to the enduring epic that tells the story of life and civilization. Years later, fortunate to be at the opening of Peter Brook's *Mahabharata* in Avignon in the South of France, I realized that Dhulku's representation to us as children was accurate and had enabled me to comprehend what was being enacted on stage even though the dialogue, written by Jean-Claude Carrière, was in French!

+

I was born in Bombay, a contemporary, open and vibrant city that was at its peak, at its very best, through the first decade of Independence. Social hierarchies were not obvious and all that mattered was what people did, and how well they did it. Merit was all. Bombay was the intellectual artery, the business

18

capital, and the cultural nerve centre of free and liberal India. Aspiration brought the young and unknown to Bombay. And then, just as I was getting firm-footed and comfortable in that wonderful, eclectic city, came Delhi and Kautilya Marg, where my grandfather had commissioned Mr Heinz, a very popular German architect, to design and build him a house. We became a 'joint family' overnight, and I began to learn the difficult and gruelling rules of give and take, of patience and adjustment.

That was fifty years ago. Our home sat on a broad and very quiet street, a radial road that ended at the edge of the Ridge, the green, untouched lung of Delhi. It felt lonely, as though we were living outside of town, in the wild, in a sterile habitat with no friendly or intrusive neighbours, no bazaars, no vendors of fruit and vegetables, no flower sellers, no nomadic minstrels, no bandarwallahs or bhaluwallahs, no kalaiwallahs or kabadiwallahs.

We did not lock our front door except at night, and then only for form's sake. Tall silver oak, jacaranda and laburnum trees guarded the lawn that was lined with flowerbeds and two tangerine trees that would fruit profusely. The memory of my grandmother's sharp and tangy 'real' bitter marmalade still makes my mouth water with longing. In the rear garden, a chicken would be decapitated for the curry or the roast, virtually every day at noon.

In the unimaginably hot months of what seemed like an unending summer laced with long hours of power cuts, we would pull out our charpais on to the large verandah, wet our sheets, wrap ourselves in the cool fabric, and surrounded by the heady fragrance of raat ki rani growing in pots along the edge of the terrace and jasmine creepers that climbed up the wall, we would fall asleep, only to awake with birdsong and sunrise. If there was a cobra in the garden, it was left alone and never killed. Snakes were a part of life in the garden. Jackals cried at the gate each night.

Images of my grandfather eating his phulka with a fork and knife, still make me laugh. He was more Anglo-Saxon than the British! A delightful man whose idea of leisure was to work hard at all that he was fascinated by. He taught himself about classical Indian art and bronzes and wrote a book called *Icons in Bronze*, he took endless photographs when he travelled and has left us iconic pictures of China in the fifties, he wrote his professional biography titled *The Morale Builders* on the Army Medical Corps that he had helped set up. He would spend hours colour-tinting black-and-white photographs of my beautiful grandmother, telling her discreetly how much he loved and cared for her. I learned what 'gracious' meant in those early years as I 'apprenticed' under his extraordinary eye and range of interests.

I remember the time he invited Zakir Husain, President of India, to tea at the house. The family had assembled to greet the exalted guest and we all sat around chatting about this, that and the other. My grandfather then brought out a handwritten Quran, the size of a matchbox or maybe even smaller, and presented it to the president. It was the most exquisite 'book' I had seen, finely crafted with its pages encased within leather bound, gilded and embossed covers. I don't think I have seen another such Quran since.

VIP trappings were considered crass and unseemly in those days. There were no clumsy security men with guns hanging about the house, being stroppy and obstreperous. Dignity accompanied presidents and prime ministers. Those were the standards they set. It was a different time. A simpler and more gracious one.

A PRICELESS LEGACY

In the fifties, there was a quiet, insular and 'protected'
New Delhi that lived alongside a vibrant, decaying
Shahjahanabad or Old Delhi as we know it today. One
'city' slept at ten, Old Delhi rocked through the night.
In many ways, these twin cities stand for an India of
then and now, confident yet confused, culturally proud
but looking to imitate that which was, at the time,
unattainable.

But I'm digressing. There was comfort in the Old
City with its crowded streets, its familiar faces, its
narrow lanes, its sounds and smells, its food and
traditional wares, its places of worship, temples,
mosques and gurudwaras, its eccentrics with their
idiosyncrasies, its iconic buildings and layers of history.

The builders of earlier centuries and eras worked
within a planned structure. Their motivation was an
entrenched pride and their aspiration was to showcase
the best of their tradition, culture, language and faith.
Ateliers produced remarkable work, local traders
marketed organic produce, musicians played, acrobats
performed, vendors serviced the residential bylanes of

the Old City. There were kite festivals, ram- and cock-fights, and a hospital for injured birds run by the Jain community. Bazaars were community 'clubs' where the men, women and children of the mohalla met and exchanged 'gossip', and news percolated through the community by word of mouth. Temples, shrines, mosques and gurudwaras lived and let live.

In the Old City, some of that ambience remains. Kinari Bazaar continues to sell silk threads, gota in gold and silver, ribbons and parandis, sehras and talwars and everything we need for festivals and weddings. Paranthewali Galli makes hot stuffed paranthas for hungry passers-by, shoppers and those who come from other parts of the city to devour this traditional specialty. Portrait photographers, using scenic—often bizarre—painted backdrops beckon you over to be photographed with the trustworthy large 'box' camera. At the base of Asia's largest mosque, the Jama Masjid, used to sit the best ever kebab shop, Masita, that would draw us to eat indescribably exquisite seekh and kakori kebabs that no other vendor has been able to match. Then one day, the bulldozers of the 'beautification of Delhi' scheme, ordered by thoughtless politicians and rootless babus, with the help of the municipal corporation pretending to 'clean up' the area, killed a treasure of the palate, an intangible legacy left to us by the Mughals. Other shops selling bits and bobs were all demolished, as were the myriad Dilliwallahs who energized the steps of the masjid. Slowly, the razed space descended into an urban slum from having been an organic cultural

33

hub of the old Muslim quarter of the city. Any other country with an iota of pride in its heritage would have conserved and nurtured its ancient roots, not worked to maul and hurt them.

Fortunately, the idiocy of our politicians and bureaucrats notwithstanding, life around Jama Masjid continues to flourish through the night. In the days of my youth, a jaunt through the labyrinthine lanes of the Old City at night would last most of the night and was an occasion of sheer joy. A late dinner at Karim's, usually a raan, leg of lamb, and istew, a stew of chops, with many rumali rotis, would mark the beginning of a walk through the gallis selling old books, posters and other memorabilia. Then would come the pose for a photograph against a painted backdrop of the Taj Mahal or a film star, before we would move on to a cup of chai, flavoured with cardamom. We would wander up to the mosque, sit on the steps and look out at the crenellated walls of the Red Fort, imagining the river beyond, the bed of which is present-day Ring Road! Amidst much laughter and conversation, we would drive to Flagstaff, Civil Lines and to the Maidens Hotel for a late night ice cream and coffee, then return to Qudsia Gardens and Chandni Chowk for hot jalebis, laced with a thick layer of malai, real cream, before heading home and to bed as dawn was breaking. That was our 'night out', our open-to-the-sky 'nightclub', introduced to me by that quintessential Dilliwallah and amusing eccentric, Akhilesh Mittal. He knew Shahjahanabad better than anyone I had met and would be his happiest self when guiding people through time and space in that part of town. It was a walk that was etched in my memory and when our son Jaisal got married decades later, it was something I recreated for wedding guests from outside the city with the help of another lover of the Old City, the writer and diplomat, Pavan Verma.

✛

When I began dating Tejbir in school, I had never been into a Sikh gurudwara. I knew nothing of rituals, Hindu or Sikh, because my mother and father were atheists and made us read about religions but never took us to places of worship other than mosques and temples of past centuries that had the blue board of the Archaeological Survey at the gate, and were not in regular use by priests and believers. Because I went to a Protestant school in Bombay, I had read the Bible, sang hymns and knew the Lord's Prayer by heart. I went to church throughout Lent, and kept a rosary under my pillow. It was the only 'religion' I was familiar with, except for one exception when Dr Karan Singh took me to the Kheer Bhawani temple in Kashmir, and where I embarrassed him and the pandit when I put out my left hand for the prasad. I knew no better in those young and carefree days. One Saturday afternoon when I went to Chandni Chowk to look for parandis in Kinari Bazaar I was drawn to the Sis Ganj shrine. It was here that Emperor Aurangzeb beheaded Guru Tegh Bahadur in November 1675 for refusing to convert to Islam.

As I stepped away from the crowded footpath and turned into the entrance of the gurudwara, I noticed running water channels in which we all washed our soiled feet before entering the sacred space. The contrast from the street to the shrine was stark. Serenity reigned within and for some unknown and obscure reason, I was intoxicated by the kirtan. I just felt good as I sat, head covered, and listened without understanding anything of what was being sung.

Believers came and bowed to the Granth Sahib, the holy book, some sat and listened to the hymns, others left. This was the religion of my future in-laws and I wanted to be initiated. I decided that day, that I would marry in the Sikh tradition, pheras and all, and not merely sign off as 'man and wife' with a registrar from the local court presiding. My parents had had a civil marriage, rare at the time, and were surprised when I announced mine would be a religious, Sikh ceremony. My father looked surprised but did not question my decision or force his views on me—I was getting married, the choice was mine.

÷

It was only recently, when chatting with Tejbir about Delhi and Shahjahanabad, that I learnt a new nugget about why Tees Hazari, which means thirty thousand, and where the law courts of modern day Delhi are now situated, came by its name. In 1783, thirty thousand Sikh troops, under the command of General Baghel Singh had crossed the river Jamuna and encamped at

this spot, preparing to enter the Red Fort. On 11
March, they stormed the Fort and occupied the Diwan-
e-Aam. The ruler then, Shah Alam II, is believed to
have negotiated with them and the quid pro quo was
that General Baghel would be permitted to build
gurudwaras on historical Sikh sites in the realm and
would also receive six annas of all octroi duties that
accrued to the Capital. That is how the gurudwara on
Chandni Chowk came to be and it was called Sis Ganj
because of the beheading of the Guru. The 'encampment'
area was named Tees Hazari, and much later, eleven
years after Independence, the foundations for the local
City Court Complex were laid.

My most vivid impressions of Old Delhi can best be
boxed into three compartments—its monuments, its
food, and its music. First, its monuments. When I
became the editor of a monthly cultural publication
called the *India Magazine*, I would fashion historic
walks in different parts of Delhi that were led by iconic
Dilliwallahs. Long before historic walks became
fashionable, Khushwant Singh would walk our groups
around Tughlakabad, Krishen Khanna would take
another lot through the scattered ruins of Jamali Kamali
at the edge of the Qutab Minar. One of the most
popular ones however was the one Akhilesh Mittal led
from Lahori Gate of the Red Fort, across the road to
the Jama Masjid and through Chandni Chowk, all the
way to Pahadi Imli, where Naseem Khan and his wife
would host the 'explorers' to an elaborate nashta of
endless delicacies, recipes of which continue to lie in the

hands of the many cooks who live in the homes, havelis and eating places in the labyrinth that is purani Dilli, that make this city a culinary delight.

Akhilesh would describe the Red Fort of Shah Jahan using his flights of vivid imagination to wrap us up in the comfort of the unseen. The covered Meena Bazaar with its luxurious wares, led to the Naqqar Khana, just at the entrance of the palace, where the drummers and the imperial band played at marked times of the day. The Diwan-e-Aam, hall of public audience was open on three sides, because the Mughals were comfortable in opulent, traditional tents with bright awnings wherever required. Beyond was the Diwan-e-Khas where the famed Peacock Throne sat till Nadir Shah plundered Dilli and took the throne with him as booty. In 1911, King George V held a durbar here. In this private area there were royal hammams, a mosque, the Rang Mahal where the Padshah Begum lived, apart from the zenana where the other queens and the women of the harem had their apartments. The nahar-i-behisht ran through the gardens, the charbagh which was called Hayat Baksh. There was an evening garden as well, the Mehtab Bagh, moonlight garden, where it is believed only flowers that blossomed at night revealed their heady fragrance till the early hours of dawn.

÷

The Jama Masjid, the largest mosque in India, was built by Shah Jahan in the late seventeenth century on a rocky outcrop, at a higher level than everything else he constructed. There are many smaller mosques in the walled city built by queens and princesses. We were introduced to the great streets that were much broader than the ones in Agra, to facilitate grand processions through the town. The road that linked the Fort with Jama Masjid was destroyed in 1857 when the British assaulted Dilli. Chandni Chowk had a canal that ran through the middle, with shops on either side, but sadly, in 1910, the canal was covered and now runs beneath the asphalt. There was a royal rest house for the weary traveller, Begum Serai, named after Roshanara Begum.

After the ransacking of Shahjahanabad in 1857, the walls of the Serai were reduced to rubble and only a small pavilion remains, testimony to its history. There was a Central Baptist church, the Sis Ganj Gurudwara, and the Sunehri Masjid that lived in harmony along that unrecognizable 'moonlit' street. When the British began to layer their buildings on the remains of the Mughal city, Colonel James Skinner built the St James Church that has recently been restored by the National Trust of India. Akhilesh would recite poems from the repertoire of Ghalib, and then translate them for us as he wove compelling images of the past that were unimaginable in the neglected and abused reality of today.

÷

Perhaps there is nothing that makes the greatness of a city more palpable than its food, and if this is the case, Delhi's greatness can be sourced back to the Old City.

malvika singh

My grandfather, who was more angrez than the angrez, would take us to eat at Moti Mahal in Daryaganj, at least once every visit during our school vacations when we were living in Bombay. I suppose it was his way of retaining his links with the real Dilli, its tandoori chicken and bheja fry. We would all pile into the car and drive through Dilli Darwaza that separated the twin cities of new and old, to this iconic restaurant. Kundan Lal, the owner, with his lush twirled moustache, wearing his trademark pathan suit, would greet my grandfather with a hearty 'Welcome General Sahib', and create a long table for the family, at a distance from the singing quawwals who for years and years sang a song I will never forget—'tere pairo pe mehndi lagi hai, aane jaane ke kabil nahin hai . . .' The standard order was tandoori chicken, kali dal and naan as the staples with delicious curried brain, grilled chops and, sometimes, butter chicken that was more Punjabi than a delicacy from the wild and rugged frontier of undivided India. Kulfi with falooda, a tasteless vermicelli, would always be the finale of the meal. Grandfather had served in the North West Frontier Agency and was addicted to its special cuisine. It was a treat for us Bombaywallahs to savour the wonderful barbequed meats of the restaurant. Many decades later, in the early years of the twenty-first century, we were invited to Moti Mahal to taste food cooked by none other than the renowned British chef, Gordon Ramsay. He had constructed an eclectic menu, worked in the traditional kitchens of Moti Mahal with its clay ovens but, alas,

30

what he churned out was no match at all to the consistently excellent fare that made Kundan Lal a star conductor of his time with a great team of sous chefs.

The other eating place that sits in a galli adjacent to the Jama Masjid is Karim's. Here, the early morning, breakfast Nihari, a marrow and meat stew, cooked overnight in fragrant spices, warm and delicious when scooped up with a roti and heartily devoured, remains an unmatched specialty. I have eaten Nihari at dawn, sitting on a wooden bench in the eatery that has been there forever. The test of its excellence is that Jaisal, a generation after me, takes off every now and again, after a late late party that ends at dawn, to savour this iconic dish before going to sleep a few hours into daybreak. The only way to eat Nihari is at the correct time, for breakfast, and not as a dinner 'dish' which has become its new avatar served up at weddings in impersonal five star hotels that are now trying to ape an Indian past, getting it wrong.

✛

And so to the music of the Old City. This was something Sheila Dhar introduced me to. She was a great singer with a deep and mellow voice that belted out nuanced emotions and gentle notes. She would sing and then relax with her paan-daan, filling her mouth with betel leaf, as she regaled me with anecdotes about her life as a singer, of the discipline of being a shagird. She would tell me about her guru, her mentors like Begum Akhtar and Siddeshwari Devi, the culture of the kotha, of the

Bais of Banaras, explain to me thumri and dadra, and opened up a new world of music for me. As a young girl growing up in Bombay in the fifties, my mother had put me through Bharatanatyam training, classical singing lessons, and yoga classes. I had fought it all because it ate into playtime and I was happier climbing trees and acting in self imagined and constructed plays. It was Sheila who ignited that sensibility in me when I was a teen.

I had not studied Indian classical music and grew up in a home where western classical music fell off the grooves of records, but the melody of whatever was playing, and the complicated movement of the scales grabbed my soul. I enjoyed listening, but have never been able to distinguish between one raga and another. Over the years, as my interest grew, the range of music I was drawn towards also grew. Sufiana, and the folk music of the desert in Rajasthan, the music of the Manganiars, has become 'habitual' listening for me. Delhi was where Amir Khushro lived, it was the centre of qawwali, of sufi music and poetry, and it is believed that the tabla, two drums played at the same time, was an invention of this city. When I was growing up, Chatur Lal was the master of the tabla. And, it was Sheila Dhar who brought the vocal musical renderings of the poetry of India into my being.

Sadly, city governments have closed the traditional spaces of mehfils, barricaded them with sullied ropes, killing the spirit of the past. Instead of great music being played in the Diwan-e-Khas and Diwan-e-Aam

32

of the Red Fort, we have had to suffer bureaucratic
cultural impositions like a son et lumière. When living
cultures are replaced with technological sound and
light spectacles, it is a sad commentary on the new
aesthetic of modern India.

'IF YOU TAMPER WITH NATURE,
NATURE WILL DESTROY YOU'

A memorable photograph taken in the early 1900s
shows three men sporting sola topis seated in a howdah
on an elephant, surveying the vast expanses of land
around the village of Malcha, looking for an appropriate
site for the new capital. They were Edwin Lutyens,
Herbert Baker and S.C. Swinton, three key players in
the building of the new imperial capital. Just behind a
gently sloping incline called Raisina Hill was the Ridge,
and initially this wilderness area had been suggested as
the possible venue for the building of the new city,
facing Shahjahanabad to its north. It was Lord Hardinge,
the Viceroy of India at the time, who argued against
that suggestion, emphatically stating: 'If you tamper
with nature, nature will destroy you'. That put an end
to the Ridge being exploited. It mercifully remains out
of reach for the builders of today who are scouting for
any and all land that meets their greedy gaze without a
care in their mind for preserving the natural environment
and ambience of Dilli.

The flat land spreading south from the village of

Malcha was punctuated with many grand and monumental edifices and tombs of past kingdoms and rulers that needed to be preserved. Finally, Raisina Hill was selected, the foundation stone laid and work began to level the peak and start the building process. Dynamite did the job and very steadily the grand, carefully formulated plan, imagined and executed by Edwin Lutyens and his partner, Herbert Baker, emerged from the foundations atop Raisina Hill. A railway track was laid to ferry the massive quantities of pink stone, which was brought from Rajasthan, to the 'off-loading station' that sat on what is today the Chelmsford Club, an institution that allowed Indians to be members, unlike the Gymkhana Club that permitted only white membership.

The team of Indians, primarily young men from five Sikh families who came to look for contracts for the building of the new capital, received the building commissions, and settled down to complete the onerous and formidable challenge they had taken on. They became the First Families of New Delhi, never to return to their homes, hearths and businesses in what became Pakistan post-Independence. Khushwant Singh, one of India's leading storytellers and author of the seminal *History of the Sikhs*, grew up in the rubble and dust of the building of New Delhi. His father, Sardar Bahadur Sobha Singh, was the lead contractor and was later knighted by the British for a job well done. He was responsible for building the forecourt of the Viceroy's Palace, now home of the president of India, Rashtrapati

Bhavan, as well as South Block that houses the offices
of the prime minister, the foreign minister and the
defence minister. He constructed India Gate, Baroda
House, Scindia House, Regal Building, Narendra Place,
some buildings in Connaught Place, residential homes
on Prithviraj Road and Sujan Singh Park among others.
With his dear friend Lala Raghubir Singh he started the
first co-educational school in the city, Modern School.
He was a pioneering entrepreneur and there are some
rather amusing stories about how his wife would
reprimand him for investing money in land and buildings
instead of buying her jewels. Sujan Singh Park was one
of those 'jewels'.

Baisakha Singh who built North Block, Dharam Singh
who supplied all the stone, and Narain Singh were the
other three who shared in the many contracts for the
new city. The chief engineer was Sir Teja Singh Malik
whose daughter married Khushwant Singh. Families
bonded, and initially, they all lived on Jantar Mantar
Road in the spacious mansions that still stand testimony
to that period in our history. Haroon al Rashid, a
contractor from Karachi, worked on Rashtrapati
Bhavan and returned to Sindh in Pakistan when his
work was completed and before India was divided.

Rashtrapati Bhavan is flanked by North and South
Blocks, which were built as offices for the Government
of India. The main avenue, Kingsway, now Rajpath,
leads down from the imposing gates of the 'palace' to
what was once called the Great Place, now Vijay Chowk,
and goes all the way down to India Gate, a memorial to

those who gave their lives in World War I. Beyond the Gate stands an empty space with four pillars holding up a cupola, under which a statue of King George V once stood. Years ago, someone in a kingdom dominated by the babu, and for reasons unknown, removed that symbol of our most recent history from its commanding position and left an emptiness under the canopy.

Fortunately, other 'remnants' of the Raj remain. I shall attempt a brief and fleeting description of the interior of Rashtrapati Bhavan because it continues to be a spectacular building that was conceived with care and love and is a fine amalgam of contrasting aesthetic sensibilities taken from the East and the West. Its architect, Edwin Lutyens, was hugely influenced by the arts and crafts movement in England and Europe. His honest, candid, often negative and unromantic, personal views about India and the Indians he met through his work here, were manifest in the building he sketched on the drawing board using all the elements that spelt 'India' for him. Imposing sandstone walls, deep verandahs bridging the inside with the outside, jaalis, chajjas, fountains, water-bodies, open-to-the-sky courtyards within the walls of the building, grand stairways, cool corridors, arched doorways, pillars embellished with bells and other elaborate carvings, fireplaces with mantles, specially designed furniture, door handles and light fixtures, all came together rather effortlessly, or so it seems from our perspective today. Carpets were woven in carefully defined patterns, different for each area, the one for the Ashoka Hall being the most eloquent in colour and design with the cypress tree as the recurring motif creating a jaal, a web, of sheer beauty, reminiscent of the valley of Kashmir. Chandeliers hung from the high ceiling that was edged by a mural. The mural had been presented to George IV of England by Fateh Ali Shah of Persia, and was never used in England. It was sent to India in 1929, when Lord Irwin was Viceroy, to embellish the high ceiling of the Ballroom at Viceroy's House. All the fabric for the upholstery and drapes was specially ordered in keeping with a subtle colour palette. There was nothing that was out of sync. That orchestra of form and colour, shape and size, façade and embellishment, was finely tuned and conducted with precision.

÷

To attend a banquet in honour of a visiting president, guests are ushered up to the first floor by an open-to-the-sky staircase, with the President's Bodyguard standing to attention, their lances at the ready, on every alternate step, till they enter the grand Ashoka Hall. A reception takes place prior to the announcement of the arrival of the President and Guest of Honour, who are heralded and introduced to each guest after which everyone is led into dinner. A formal table setting, in the grand dining room for a sit-down presidential banquet, is the norm even today. A butler stands behind every guest each of whom is seated in keeping with protocol. The formal service of 'courses' happens according to the menu placed atop each place setting. Speeches are delivered and piped music plays throughout the meal. Gold Coin apple juice is served for the official toast instead of champagne, as the Indian state abjures alcohol.

At one such evening that my husband and I were privileged to attend, he with his flowing white beard, was chatting with a group of people at the far end of the room. I was with Najma Heptullah, then the Deputy Speaker of the Rajya Sabha. Her eyes wandered away from me as she spoke about various things rather animatedly as is her wont. Suddenly she said, 'I will just be back, Mala, must go and say hello to Barnala Sahib.' I turned to see where Barnala, a politician from Punjab, was and found she had spotted Tejbir in the far corner and thought he was Barnala. It was the only 'funny' interlude during an otherwise dull dinner party because I was seated at the tail of the table, low in protocol, and having to chat with the ADC of a visiting dignitary from a European nation who spoke not a word of English.

On another occasion, President and Mrs Narayanan had a private farewell dinner party in the Yellow Drawing Room for Gopal Gandhi who had served as the president's secretary. The guest list was a wonderful mix of Gopal's friends, and the mood was relaxed and happy. It was so relaxed that I virtually scolded the president for missing the deadline of an article he had promised to write for *Seminar*, the magazine my parents had founded, and that Tejbir and I continue to edit.

A Naga band played as we ate off silver thaalis. It was unusual, special and memorable to be able to have a quiet, informal dinner with a president.

When our dear friend Pavan Varma was Press Secretary to President Shankar Dayal Sharma, the Babri Masjid had just been brought down and a delegation of us appalled and deeply pained citizens, walked up Raisina Hill to meet the president and register our anger that such an illegal act could happen in broad daylight with the state looking on and doing nothing to ensure the protection of a monument. When I spoke to President Sharma about the shame of what had happened, tears began to roll down his cheeks and he said that he was as disturbed and upset about the demolition as we were. That stumped me and I could say nothing more.

There were stories from earlier times told to us by friends who were ADCs to the other presidents. One anecdote stands out. Mrs Giri, wife of President V.V. Giri, was drying her hair in the traditional way by lying on a string cot with burning coals beneath it, smoking the moisture out of her locks, when the fire alarm went off and there was momentary panic till the staff realized it was nothing serious, only a hair drying exercise. In those days the ADCs would have parties by the poolside. I was invited to one and arrived with my swimsuit rolled in a towel, all set for a midnight swim, to find the other women guests dressed to the gills in chiffon saris with brocade borders, as if for a wedding reception. I stayed in the water the entire evening.

The other 'public' events hosted by the president each year are receptions and the At Home, held on Independence Day, 15 August, and Republic Day, 26 January, in the Mughal Gardens laid out meticulously by Lutyens who was very influenced by Gertrude Jekyll, a garden designer who had ingrained in him a profound respect for flowers, plants, trees and shrubs. The gardens are beautiful, and both these garden parties are utterly charming affairs where high tea is served and where the 'rulers' of India meet with ordinary professionals, albeit those privileged enough to be invited. There was a time when bands played as people mingled easily with one another. The sad difference today is that the VIPs are caged within a rope cordon, while the guests float about aimlessly, disconnected from their host. The once tactile event of an At Home that Dilliwallahs looked forward to, has become a cold and sterile occasion.

Beyond the wrought iron gates of Rashtrapati Bhavan stand North and South Blocks. These buildings were designed by Herbert Baker and were placed on a higher plinth than the foundation of the 'Palace'. Parliament House sits below the incline in its circular frame on the left of North Block, at the edge of Vijay Chowk. Baker and Lutyens argued endlessly and vociferously about the shape of that building and in the end, Lutyens won. He had wanted the building to be round while Baker had wanted a half hexagon. Since Connaught Place was in the round, so to speak, it made sense to abide by the circular form for continuity in the larger architectural scheme.

There was a time, in the not so distant past, when I looked forward to my visits to Parliament to listen to the Budget being presented. There was a sanctity and formality that infused the House and it was an honour to sit in the Speaker's Gallery. I savour the memory of those moments when I compare the 'then' to the shameful and crude pandemonium that invades the same space 'now'. We were the generation that had seen the best of India post Independence, the highs and the lows and then the reinvention of the country and the city. The last few years have been distressing and shameful as we, as a nation, have permitted the political and administrative 'castes' that rule our lives today, to dismantle our precious institutions by their unabashed disrespect for what our founding fathers had created.

42

✢

Other landmarks and buildings of importance in the imperial city include Teen Murti House, once the residence of the Commander-in-Chief, which at Independence became the official residence of Jawaharlal Nehru, India's first prime minister, and was converted into a museum and library upon his death. On the rotary in front of the residence stands a cenotaph that celebrates the battle of Haifa, the last Imperial Service Cavalry charge on 23 September 1918 which is still celebrated today by the Indian army as Haifa Day. The Teen Murtis represent a dismounted sowar from each of the regiments that took part in the charge—the Jodhpur Lancers who led it, the Hyderabad Lancers and the Mysore Lancers. These three regiments were a part of the Imperial Service Troops. Today, they have been amalgamated into a single mounted regiment, the 61st Cavalry.

The Princely States of India were given land around Rajpath to build their palaces when New Delhi was planned. Of them, Hyderabad House, when taken over by the Indian government at Independence, was redesigned for all official bilateral meetings and banquets held in honour of visiting heads of state; Jaipur House became the Museum of Modern Art. These are the only two that stand with a semblance of dignity. Sadly, most of the others have been misused and mutilated. Baroda House and Patiala House, both splendid buildings of that period, have been defaced and demeaned by government departments—the railways and the lower courts respectively. Once upon a time I had suggested that all the 'palaces' on the India Gate roundabout should be converted into national museums—Baroda House as the Museum of Indian Medical Sciences as well as Astronomy, and Patiala House as the Museum of the Skills of the Hands. We could have created a public space to showcase the 'best of India' and have had wonderful food shacks selling the country's diverse and extraordinary cuisine. Nothing came of it. The unimaginative babu and the careless political class disregarded many ideas that came their way.

Spreading out from the base of Raisina Hill were the homes for the officers of the government, built in relation and proportion to their position and office. Large

43

sprawling bungalows with enormous gardens were for
the senior civil servants and smaller establishments for
the deputies, the assistants, the clerks and other
employees. The houses were all whitewashed and
sparkled in the Indian sun. The horticultural input was
staggering, with thousands of trees and a vast variety
of creepers, bushes and flowers, carefully planted within
a perfect grid. Sundar Nursery, at the edge of
Nizamuddin, was the home where saplings were
nurtured and from where they were distributed. Much
has been destroyed over the past decades but recently,
Ratish Nanda, a conservation architect who represents
the Aga Khan Foundation, is restoring that sprawling
tract of land where forgotten edifices of past empires
lie. It is one of the few successful heritage projects in the
city, and it is to be hoped that in the next decade or so,
some of the glories of Delhi will rise again, resplendent.

44

A GRACIOUS TOWN

Strictly speaking, although this might mark me out as a pedant, 'New Delhi', as opposed to North, South, East and West Delhi, is defined by spacious bungalows, set behind large lawns outlined with deep hedges to buffer the sounds of cars and horns; broad roads with jamun, neem, laburnum and jacaranda trees; rotaries breaking the monotony of the endless asphalt grid of the city; no ugly high-rise buildings at all; only the occasional baoli and tomb establishing past supremacy and residence—Safdarjung, Humayun, the Lodhis, Nizamuddin Auliya.

Nizamuddin is an urban village within the city. It is a Lal Dora area like many others—Masjid Moth, Shahpur Jat and more—villages that once lay along the route into Delhi from Agra. The Mughal emperor had ordered there be no disturbance to indigenous settlements en route, when his army marched here to establish the capital and build Shahjahanabad on the banks of the Jamuna. Different identities had to be protected. A lal dora or red rope, was thus draped around the periphery of such 'villages' and they were untouched by the new invader, preserved by the developers of yore. Today, with the exception of 'Lutyens' Delhi' where powerful politicians and wealthy industrialists live, and a couple of other Lal Dora areas like Nizamuddin and Shahpur Jat which have successfully reinvented themselves, most Lal Dora areas, bypassed as they are by municipal laws and regulations, wallow in neglect.

Any examination of the modern city in a biography of this length, cannot hope to do justice to its vastness and complexity, so I intend to limit myself to the areas I know best—its centre, and the southern fringe, areas I have lived and rambled in for much of my growing years. Besides Lutyens' Delhi and the great buildings of the imperial city that I have described in the previous chapter, in the early decades of its development, New Delhi was a fairly well planned city. Take Chanakyapuri. Also called Diplomatic Enclave, since it was earmarked for the diplomatic corps, it was the only 'planned' space post Lutyens' Delhi. It was conceived carefully, laid down on a grid with artery roads intersecting the main avenue, Shanti Path, the path of peace. Sixty years later, it remains one of the most luxurious avenues in the city, with broad borders of green turf lining a tarred four-lane street that eventually intersects the Ring Road, built nearly fifty years ago as an 'expressway', skirting the outer city boundaries, linking Old and New Delhi from the 'outside' in.

Gradually, as Chanakyapuri grew and developed into a new colony, other houses came up on Kautilya Marg where we lived. As the embassies on either side of Shanti Path became operational and the residential

46

colony on Malcha Marg attached itself to Diplomatic Enclave, stores opened and traditional 'specialists' found their way to our homes and soon became familiar faces in the larger, extended family. Slowly and steadily the cultural ethos of Dilli had started to enter New Delhi.

South End Lane was where 'Lutyens' Delhi' ended, flanked by Lady Willingdon Garden, now Lodhi Garden. Sujan Singh Park was considered to be on the edge of the city as was Khan Abdul Gaffar Khan Market, Khan Market today, built on the graveyards of past empires. The ghosts, upon whose spaces we now live, continue to visit us with their curious but benign presence!

Built by Sir Sobha Singh, Sujan Singh Park's seven apartment blocks placed around two quadrangles, faced each other across what was Cornwallis Road. Rising exactly ninety-one feet, aligned with the tree line, the high-ceilinged flats are sensibly designed and encircled with deep verandahs that keep them cool in the summer and are great sit-outs during the crisp and sunny winter. They remain among the most coveted homes in the city, in the core area of New Delhi, within walking distance of the stunning Lodhi Garden at one end and the Purana Qila at the other. Khan Market is next door, as is the Golf Club where the course is embellished by decaying tombs of past empires. Mature trees, sentinels of bygone times and the present, cast their shadows on those fortunate to live in this part of town.

I was privileged to marry one of Sir Sobha Singh's grandsons, Tejbir, and moved into Sujan Singh Park, the family's residential bastion. Four generations of this large and rambling First Family of New Delhi live in their 'nuclear' spaces, under one large roof, always there for each other when the need arises, but independent in their individual flats. There is no other comfort as reassuring as this togetherness without having to abide by a strict set of rules that govern similar sprawling joint families. Family links abide and a sense of being rooted in the city gets passed on through the generations. Someone described the extended family perfectly when she said: 'When young Jaisal returns home after a weekend party and tumbles into bed at four in the morning and turns off his lights, Chacha Khushwant Singh, his grand-uncle, turns his on to begin another day!'

Further afield is Meherchand Market, a South Delhi bazaar where my grandmother had a tailor who stitched her sari blouses and petticoats. The dyers were there, too—Punjab Dyers are still in the same space, spilling out on to the corridor. For many decades they have been the best in the business and they are still much in demand—they do the best ever steam press in town. Local markets have been an abiding aspect of this city. The basic needs of people living in the many colonies that make up the city are taken care of by them. There is always a fruit and vegetable store, a sweetmeat shop, a streetfood dhaba, a grocery store, a chemist, a flower vendor, a cloth store, a tailor, a drycleaner, a shoe shop and a hardware store with an electrician on call. Colonies were self-sufficient. Going shopping to Connaught Place or Dariba was more like an excursion, a day out.

Today, Meherchand Market, and nearby Lodi Colony Market, are being reinvented as are much of New Delhi's colony markets with a bunch of high-quality new restaurants run by young trained chefs offering personalized services; fashion retail outlets, such as those of designers Manish Arora and Rajesh Pratap; boutiques selling baby clothes for a new generation; bookshops and accessories stores. Then there are cafes, a shop selling a mindboggling variety of teas; The Altitude Store, an organic food store run by Ayesha Grewal, a young entrepreneur who sources the best products from across the country; specialty grocers selling every conceivable variety of frozen seafood, on one end of the spectrum, to Middle Eastern cooking ingredients at the other. The young Dilliwallahs are making new demands on the market. Their tastes are becoming eclectic and international, forcing a wide diversity of organic products and merchandise to enter the marketplace.

In our time, when my husband and I set up home in Sujan Singh Park in the seventies, there was an enterprising duo, K.D. Singh, an old Dilli 'boy' from Baird Road off Connaught Place, and Kuldeep Shankar, who launched the first 'food store', Steakhouse, in a laid-back colony called Jor Bagh. The products stacked on shelves that reached the ceiling were all that was unavailable in other shops. Cheese of many types, cold cuts, cans of Mexican chillies, soft toilet paper unlike the sandpaper variety we had grown up with, Tabasco and HP Sauce, apart from boring old tomato ketchup

49

and lots more, made this shop a weekly one-stop destination. It has survived the onslaught of competition that came with the country's economy being liberalized in the 1990s and we continue to go there every Saturday morning—it's our personal shopping ritual. I eat my favourite ham sandwiches there, with dollops of mustard, sitting in the rear room that doubles up as a store and office. Kullu, the old faithful behind the counter suggests products and recipes, as does Bir Singh, grey and aging, but still able to recall the favourites of all the loyal customers—'aap ka taaza Brie aa gaya hai!'

Sharing a common wall with Steakhouse is The Bookshop, still run by KD and his gentle, delightful wife, Nini. One of them is always there no matter how dire the weather. The couple read and love books, making browsing there a joy. On the weekend you invariably meet friends stopping by to see what is new on the shelves, or to find out which titles KD is recommending. I have a long and special relationship with The Bookshop and when desperate to buy a gift, I ask KD on the phone, whether the person would like this or that book or what he would suggest. More often than not he is right in his judgement, especially as he has a phenomenal memory and knows exactly who has read what! The clients of The Bookshop and Steakhouse range from prime ministers to ordinary mortals like us. Both these men deserve keys to the city for quality and perseverance, for being pioneers, 'selling' the toughest products at a time when customers for eclectic food products and books, were few and far between. They befriended all and are a part of the landscape of New Delhi.

Yet they are the sort of people Delhi keeps throwing up for it is a city which has always nurtured people who are out of the ordinary. It is rare to find someone who will make 150 food packages and distribute them to homeless dogs. Bhim and Rita are one such couple. The story goes that Rita had begun to feed four dogs that lived on the streets around her home in Sujan Singh Park. One day she had to leave for Assam on work and asked her husband, who had been groaning about the additional household expense of feeding the four dogs, to give them their daily bread on her behalf. I have to say here that Rita worked at the time with Mother Teresa and did so very silently, because in the evenings after work in the slums of Delhi, she would don her fine French chiffons, clip stunning earrings onto her earlobes and venture out into the la-di-da dinner parties of the rich and mighty. Bhim agreed to feed the dogs in the absence of his wife and before he knew it he had fallen in love with the strays and had added fourteen more dogs to the rolls. In just a short while he was feeding, inoculating and looking after 120 dogs, and that list continued to expand. The dogs know when their dinner will be delivered to them and stand on the pavements in and around Khan Market and Lodhi Gardens, waiting patiently for their sustenance. Generous and chilled out Bhim was loved by us all and when he passed on, rather suddenly and without

51

warning, Rita carried on his endeavour and has now taken the number of food packages to 170. Where in the world can one expect to find this kind of sheer 'giving'?

That was also the time when Fabindia made its presence felt in the retail space. John Bissell, the founder, and Riten Mazumdar, a designer from Shantiniketan in Bengal, settled in Delhi, had helped my mother with upholstery and curtains when she was doing up her cottage at the rear of the large family home on Kautilya Marg. Gentle Riten hand-painted the curtains for our room on natural raw silk bought from Khadi Gram Udyog and John produced endless swatches of handloom fabric for the sofa and chairs, cushion covers and bedspreads. Years later, Terence Conran, who started the Habitat chain of stores in England, came to Delhi, and with John, sourced all the rugs and durries for his store from Panipat, from Madhukar Khera. John was a pioneer in his field and set a trend that is vibrant and alive today. Many years later I converted those 'Riten' curtains into trousers for myself.

÷

The rather more distinctive enclaves in South Delhi are residential housing developments which were developed on the lines of modern-day professional 'guilds'. And so Niti Bagh became the lawyers' colony; Chittaranjan Park, once referred to as East Pakistan Displaced Persons' (EPDP) colony is where Bengalis are in the majority; Mayfair Gardens is where the Sindhis went;

Vasant Vihar and Shantiniketan became a haven for retired babus; Defence Colony, by definition was an enclave for defence personnel; and so on.

So much for the physical contours of New Delhi as it once was, and as it continued to be for the first few decades of its development, before it was overtaken by the blight of unplanned development of which we will see more in the second section of this book.

÷

New Delhi was once a gracious town. A quiet elegance was its hallmark. An austere sensibility dictated the dress sense of men and women who knew instinctively what was right and what was over the top. The homes of the professionals and of wealthy businessmen were never ostentatious or extravagant, instead they were comfortable, happy, personal spaces where no one felt intimidated. Family heirlooms and hand-me-downs as well as souvenirs bought on trips and vacations, were the objects displayed in the living areas, interspersed with family pictures in silver frames and portraits of ancestors on the walls.

Entertainment and dinner parties in those days were at home. There were no 'caterers' bar one—Greens, who did wedding teas and dinners. Anything larger than a sit-down dinner was a cocktail party with drinks and an array of eats. I remember my grandmother sitting at our large dining table preparing canapés for a party, my favourite being Monaco biscuits heaped with sardine paste and a dot of ketchup. All manner of exotic cocktails, ingeniously concocted by my grandfather and his potent imagination, were rigorously shaken in a cocktail shaker and then ceremoniously poured out into elegant, appropriate glasses. The 'bearer' of the house, dressed in a white bandgala with a turrah as his headgear, would make the rest of the drinks. No one ever used outside caterers, as is the wont today. Women came dressed for the occasion. The cocktail party crowd wore French chiffon saris embellished with Banarasi brocade borders, a fine mix of Indian and Western styles. Pearls were fashionable as cocktail party jewellery. The real heavy stuff came out of the bank locker at weddings. The men wore a dress suit or a bandgala, a sherwani or a regular lounge suit. It all appeared rather formal, but was invariably loads of fun, with repertoires of jokes and laughter invading the evening. People looked good and felt good. It was 'goodbyes' by nine. Since there was no television in those days, we would catch the end of the nine o' clock All India Radio news bulletin, eat our soup in the drawing room and then stroll in the garden dissecting the party before falling into bed.

The sit-down dinners were far more structured. All the formal crockery and cutlery had to be cleaned and polished. The table had to be laid perfectly, candles and all. Flowers had to be arranged. Bulbs in lamps had to be checked inside the house and outside. It took two days to organize a dinner for twelve or twenty. Cards went out with an RSVP. Guests arrived bang on time. The conversation was always engaging, but no matter

54

how engrossing, it would be interrupted at the exact hour by the call to dinner. Place cards ensured compatibility with the persons on your right and left as well as those opposite you, and post a four-course Western meal, everyone moved from the dining room back to the drawing room for coffee, cognac, liqueurs and chocolates. This was the drill in the more Westernized homes or 'army' families. The 'buffet' of today—standing about with plates full of food, trying to balance fork and knife as well as a glass of wine and enjoy the meal—was once considered unacceptable for a 'dinner' party. It was clumsy and unappetizing. As a people, we Indians have always preferred to sit and eat whether from thaalis or plates or on banana leaves. Eating has always been a ritual, almost a spiritual rite.

I recall some splendid dinners through the sixties of the last century at the Charat Ram home on Sardar Patel Marg, then called Kitchener Road. Charat Ram and Bharat Ram were sons of Lala Shri Ram who was the head of one of Delhi's most influential business clans. Their homes were adjacent to one another—Lal Kothi was where the Bharat Rams lived and Chhabees Number was the Charat Ram residence, a home where the table was always set with gleaming silver thaalis and many katoris filled with delectable vegetables and dals. Rice and puris, rotis and 'seconds' were served. It was hysterically amusing to see people eat with a fork and knife from a thaali while we ate with our fingers, savouring the delicate spices and fresh chilli pickle, drowned in sesame seeds and mustard oil. There were

55

no drinks before or after dinner. Things have since changed. Drinks are now served before dinner, the thaalis are dulled with the patina of times past, but the wonderful vegetarian food has only become better.

Down the road from the Charat Ram and Bharat Ram mansions, lived Clovis Maksud, ambassador of the Arab League of States. His was an unforgettable embassy where guests ranging from Indira Gandhi and Krishna Hutheesing to journalists and filmmakers, poets and painters, socialites and bureaucrats, all came together for an evening of good conversation, delicious Middle Eastern food and new connections. Maksud dominated the diplomatic scene, surpassing the ambassadors of Britain and the United States, who in the heady days of Non-Alignment and Panchsheel, were not feted by the Indian establishment. Those from the Middle East, the Soviet Union, Yugoslavia and China were top of the pops. I remember the visit of Chinese prime minister, Chou en Lai, to Delhi in 1960 with us children lining the roads waving flags and chanting 'Hindi-Chini bhai bhai' as the open motorcade drove by en route to Rashtrapati Bhavan where visiting heads of state would stay. We loved China.

The wife of the Chinese ambassador, Mrs Ma, if I remember correctly, set an elaborate table and served the most memorable and elegant feasts at the residence that sat in all its splendour on Shanti Path. It was the first to come up on 'embassy row'! She taught my mother how to cook a range of wonderful, unusual dishes. Prawns tossed lightly in rice flour and then put into bubbling, hot peanut oil for one minute flat, not a second longer, were the most succulent I have ever eaten. Sweet and Sour sauce was not ketchup with a few tablespoons of chemically made vinegar but instead, a mixture of real tomato puree, a bit of sugar and a dash of Chinese rice vinegar, with a lacing of chillies and finely shredded capsicum to enhance the flavour of the sauce. She would cut all the ingredients in different shapes and sizes for each dish, stand them in glass bowls along the wall of the chopping table, and create one dish after another by cooking meat, fish, vegetables, tofu and more, for a minute each in a wok. Chinese food at her home, and later, at my mother's table, was nothing like the Punjabified Chinese cuisine at the many restaurants in Delhi.

Amongst the more authentic restaurants was Ginza, in the outer circle of Connaught Place. It was a small, narrow corridor-like room at the end of which sat a large, fat Chinese gentleman who ran the show. The food was delicious and it became the regular haunt for journalists like Girilal Jain and Shamlal, filmmakers like Shanti Chowdhury visiting from Calcutta, and many others. My father and mother were often at Ginza, having animated conversations with their friends over large bowls of Talumein soup and pork spare-ribs.

÷

This was the time when Delhi University had extraordinary faculty. In the intellectual ferment of post independence India, a host of brilliant young economists, sociologists and political scientists were starting their long trajectory of intellectual eminence. There was a sense of the 'adda' when I went along with my parents to visit Mrinal Dutta Chowdhury, P.N. Dhar and others in Old Delhi where they lived in close proximity to the campus. It was here that Nobel Laureate Amartya Sen taught. In fact, I recall he wrote for the magazine in *Seminar*'s first year. Andre Beteille, the grand man of sociology, Raj Krishna of the 'Hindu rate of growth' fame, Sukhamoy Chakravarty and a host of others energized the university at the time. Most went on to make a huge impact on thought and policy.

Seminar was a forum for these men and women to share their new ideas with a larger community of readers, students and policymakers across India. Our office in Malhotra Building, on the edge of Janpath where it joins the inner circle of Connaught Place, soon became a central meeting place for a fascinating and diverse group of professionals and individuals, much like our home in Bombay had been, since that home, too, had doubled up as an office. Lunch came from home in a tiffin carrier, as it continues to do, and whoever dropped by, ate with us. Newspaper editors and columnists like Girilal Jain and Shamlal, both editors of the *Times of India*; Nikhil Chakravarthy who edited *Mainstream*, a left of centre weekly magazine; Ajit Bhattacharji and more; cartoonists like Abu Abraham; painters like J. Swaminathan, Krishen Khanna; writers like Balwant Gargi and Mulk Raj Anand, who had moved to Delhi by then; Patwant Singh who edited a magazine called *Design*, peopled our lives. My parents reached out to many young students and academics as well. I was first introduced to Montek Singh Alhuwalia, Pavan Varma, Vir Sanghvi, to name a few, by my father. As young teenagers, my brother Valmik and I were always included in the group and the conversation.

Near the *Seminar* office was another adda that gave the city its intellectual energy—the Indian Coffee House, where politicos, journalists and concerned, caring citizens met over coffee and greasy vegetable cutlets, to exchange news and gossip, to critique the happenings in the country, to argue and debate, and just have a great time chatting about everything under the sun. The iconic Coffee House of my time is dead and gone. It was transplanted to Baba Kharak Singh Marg opposite Mohan Singh Place but none of the old charm remained. Today, it has been replaced by Café Coffee Days across the city where no one knows anyone, where you have your coffee and scoot off to another mindless meeting.

For, although we did not know it at the time, the city was about to have its heart ripped out of it, the Dil would go out of Dilli as soulless babus, avaricious builders, grubby money-men, and corrupt politicians would 'destroy' the ethos of the city once and for all in the name of progress, regulations, and modernization.

SECTION II

CHANGING CITY

CHANGING CITY

In the old days, as one passed through Dilli Darwaza and headed towards India Gate, from the Red Fort to Raisina Hill, you would feel as if you were being cut off from life itself as you moved away from Shahjahanabad's noisy chaos to the broad expansive boulevard of Kingsway that chained Rashtrapati Bhavan to India Gate. After Independence, Kingsway became Rajpath, an equally pompous name that reinforced, symbolically, the carefully ordered social and economic 'layers' that were the hallmarks of the new city that the British had built and bequeathed to us when they departed. Queensway, now called Janpath, path of the people, the avenue of the aam aadmi, intersects its 'male' counterpart at its central axis, flanked by the National Museum and the National Archives, leading on further to Connaught Place, and beyond, to Jama Masjid at the heart of Shahjahanabad, bridging the two distinctly different hearts of Dilli. One that ticks for the rulers, and the other for the ruled!

As you drove along Janpath, the first arresting building you would come to was Scindia House, bequeathed to Khushwant Singh and his brother Gurbux by Sir Sobha Singh. Here on the ground floor, opening on to Janpath, sat the famous jeweller, Kanjimull, and the great silver shop, Cooke and Kelvey. Further down the corridor was the leading optician, Lawrence and Mayo, and next to it, the Delhi Safe Deposit, where the grand jewels of the wealthy were kept in safe custody.

Across the road is the Cottage Industries Emporium, a one-stop-destination for crafts from across India. The best and most beautiful of handcrafted products and woven fabrics and saris were stocked there. Outside it was a café-cum-bookshop, one of the first in Delhi, called Bankura, named after the terracotta horse from Bankura in Bengal. It is no more. Cottage, as it was referred to, was tucked behind a row of makeshift shops on Janpath that sold all manner of wares. We came here regularly to match blouses with saris, pyjamas with kurtas. We bought chappals and bags, supari and saunf, and 'artificial' jewellery as it was called in those days. Around the corner was Khadi Gram Udyog that sold brightly coloured kurtas, the mainstay of every young person's wardrobe during the sixties and seventies. And a few metres beyond was Hanuman Mandir, temple of the Monkey God, where on Tuesday each week, the bangle and flower-sellers would set up shop. We all wore dozens of those translucent glass bangles on our arms and different coloured bindis on our foreheads to match our clothes.

During the fifties and the sixties, Connaught Place,

the grand pillared shopping arcade, housed the best of India. Many of the familiar shops that were all the rage at the time have disappeared, but the thought of them and their stunning products, brings forth a strange kind of yearning. Glamour was where many of my generation bought saris for their trousseau; when avocados were unheard of in Delhi, they could be found at Oriental Fruit Mart as were the amazing bulls-eye sugar sweets; Harnarain Gopinath had a mind-boggling assortment of sherbets, murabbas and pickles; the lone bookstore was Galgotias; the best chemist, Sahib Singh; Greenways was the haberdashery and Jainsons the one store for 'readymade' clothes and cashmere cardigans; it was from Finlays that all the stylish Sikh men bought their turban lengths; MR Stores had every conceivable piece of hardware; Chinese Art Palace was where one rummaged around for that special something in blue-and-white pretending to be a Ming vase.

Then one day a rather ugly, concrete high-rise building poked through the low and calm skyscape. It was called Super Bazaar, the dream child of a then young Gandhian, Laxmi Jain, where daals, an assortment of grains, rice and spices, vegetables and fruit, basic household appliances and suchlike, were available under one roof and, most critically, at reasonable prices with a guarantee of quality. It was the city's first supermarket. It exists no more. The other 'high-rise' structure that triggered many more to follow, was the Life Insurance Corporation building at the edge of the outer circle of Connaught Place, designed by Charles Correa, a Bombay

65

architect of great repute. Many of us Dilliwallahs saw it as a monstrosity that was ruining our spacious and structured town centre. Soon, Statesman House joined the building race and before we could absorb the shock of the first tremors of this radical overhaul, downtown Delhi was going through the contractions of the 'high-rise' boom and a litter of tall, angular buildings were being born. All potential fire hazards. Connaught Place remained at the heart of this concrete maze, sparkling white, amidst walls of grey.

The radial roads that struck out and away from the central circle were reminders of a pre-Independence period. Curzon Road, named after the viceroy who orchestrated the shift of the capital from Calcutta to Delhi, that connected India Gate to Connaught Place, was a tree-lined road with large residential bungalows wrapped in beautifully turfed open spaces. It all changed dramatically when the name of the road became Kasturba Gandhi Marg. High-rise buildings with no contemporary architectural message, surrounded by dirty, broken-down entrances devoid of trees and evergreen bushes, smelly and unkempt, established the aesthetic of a 'new' India trying desperately to be what it was not. Residential areas were usurped by ugly commercial office blocks. The trees vanished and with them the oxygen of a living culture.

Another such memorable street was Irwin Road where fruit and vegetable vendors sold their fresh and delicious products, displayed on stands that sloped down from a height to waist level, a visual treat that could be defined as an art 'installation'. It was typical of all Indian fruit and vegetable stalls in all towns and cities. When Irwin Road was renamed Baba Kharak Singh Marg, the ambience and mood experienced a metamorphosis. State handicrafts shops sprouted, housed in ugly concrete buildings, far removed from the organic, living and breathing products within. A strange 'modernization', that of the babu, was beginning to usurp the city. Modern it was not, because it had not grown out of an indigenous, local idiom, but from Corbusier's cold and calculated style of static, inflexible architectural forms using a horrible material called reinforced concrete. It does not breathe easily; it is heavy in weight and absorbs every odour. Real India is uncomfortable without tactility, colour, noise and human chaos, all jostling together with unaffected abandon. We do not know how to handle frigid and rigid structures. It goes against our cultural imagination.

÷

A new 'builder' had reared its head—the Delhi Development Authority (DDA). Established in 1957, it became obviously active from 1967 onwards. The name itself was undemocratic, unfriendly, anti-city, anti-people. It was an 'authority', and heaven help you if you questioned it. Heavy-handed, uninitiated in the nuances of architectural styles and the past's delicate aesthetic sensibilities, the men who ruled the roost from then to now have surely and steadily uprooted and destroyed this fine, fragile and layered ancient city as they raced to create the modern middle-class slums that surround us. These 'habitats' are alien spaces, disconnected with the ethos and idea of India and Bharat.

Worse was to come. The last time the city was deliberately brutalized was by the hand of foreigners in 1857 when Britons vandalized Shahjahanabad. This time we suffered at the hands of our own. During the Emergency, Sanjay Gandhi decided to clear slums and 'beautify' areas and used the then chairman of the DDA, Shri Jagmohan, to do his bidding. What followed was possibly the worst ever assault on the people who lived in the historic environs of Purani Dilli. Jagmohan rolled the bulldozers across the Ramlila Maidan and demolished Turkman Darwaza, one of the imposing gates of Shahjahanabad, for no rhyme or reason. Ancestral family homes and havelis were razed to the ground and abjectly poor families, who had settled in the surrounding areas, were relocated to the flood plain of the Jamuna, only to suffer each year as their makeshift shacks were submerged during the monsoon. Diseases ravaged the slums. Old Dilliwallahs, proud descendants of the Mughals, suffered in pained silence. They, as the rightful keepers of that enduring legacy, had been alienated, divorced from their roots and insulted.

Images of that 'authority' still make one's hair stand on end. We hoped and prayed that Dilli Darwaza, Mori Darwaza, Kashmiri Darwaza and the others, would not be put through similar humiliation. Our city had been mutilated by our own. We had learned no lessons from history. The 'respect' for the local communities by a conquering Mughal power in the past had made life inclusive, creating the palpable, living ethos of Dilli. The tragedy is that the modern Indian state post 1947 disregarded that tradition. The 'authority' knew no better as it demolished a valuable chunk of history. It lost the respect of the people over whom it had been mandated to wield its authority, without a by your leave, and it has not been successful in winning the respect back. Land grab, extortion, blackmail and corruption ensued and the land and civic authorities continued to exploit the citizens of this ancient city.

Dilli had begun to lose her many past identities and her ancestry at the heavy hand of the DDA, and two other uncoordinated fingers, the two municipalities— the New Delhi Municipal Corporation (NDMC) and the Municipal Corporation of Delhi (MCD). All of them claim jurisdiction over the city, but are quick to evade responsibility when having to deal with its problems.

We just do not know how to conserve and be proud of what is ours. We have no sense of wanting to be custodians of our legacies for our children. Having mutilated its space, its buildings, its traditional street food, its bazaars and its energy, India today is seeking World Heritage status for Delhi. Shahjahanabad— honoured in international capitals with great exhibitions on its people, art and culture—well deserves that valued status, but sadly, those municipalities and authorities who have been responsible for the city's management and administration for over six decades since Independence have failed to deliver what the city should have been able to take for granted. A knotted criss-cross of wires overhead, open drains, unmanageable traffic with every type of vehicle fighting for space, illegal encroachments, decaying and unsafe buildings, all come together in a tangled mess.

Lutyens' Delhi had been a low-rise area, a garden city, till one day, the Fonseca Hotel, on one end of Mansingh Road, was sold off, with all the old trees, sentinels of past secrets, that had once littered its spacious grounds, to the Taj Group of Hotels that was desperate for a presence in the Capital City. An unexpected permission to break the prevailing mandated height norm for a building, was given to them, allegedly negotiated by Rukhsana Sultana, a cousin-in-law of my husband's. It was rumoured she did it through the good offices of Sanjay Gandhi. The powerful and mighty had intervened and rubbished their 'own' prescribed law. The irregular 'deal' was transacted, and a sore thumb punctured the pristine skyline of a conservation area, the newest lung of Delhi, second to the Ridge that Lord Hardinge had preserved for the future of this city. The deadly nexus of 'politics, commerce and the administration' had together made its first foray into a realm that was, till then, seen to be relatively devoid of inappropriate practice. The city began to change yet again.

Delhi, beyond what Lutyens had built, was gradually

becoming a much larger town, a small city. Real estate was beginning to boom. Seeing many lucrative opportunities in this changing habitat, errant and corrupt municipalities looked the other way when rules were being battered and taking bribes for permitting gross illegalities was becoming the norm. The Urban Affairs ministry, as well as all the other related departments concerned, did not intervene either, despite witnessing the degrading horror unfold. Encroachments were ignored for a 'price', as all the colonies were choked and abused. Seeing this happen, the ancient urban villages within this modern, spreading city, preserved by the protective Lal Dora of the invading armies of the Mughals, started to smell the coffee and possible profit and commerce. Encouraged by the fact that no general municipal rules and regulations applied to them, they began replacing ancient, low-rise structures with narrow high-rise buildings, all constructed in a haphazard, unplanned manner, adhering to no safety norms. No one objected. Delhi was being sacked yet again.

÷

Fortunately, it wasn't all bad. There was change that was good, there was even change that was great. Decades before the DDA and other such authorities rode roughshod over the state of Delhi, there was a happy energy and carefree vitality in this city that was infectious. The first crop of private entrepreneurs were opening shop despite archaic regulatory mechanisms that seemed to want to defeat enterprise. Government servants were always around, asking for their 'hafta' that had become the easy way of receiving some loose cash. They were suffocating the city but equally, the 'flower generation' of the sixties was not to be held back or contained.

The Tea House, at the corner of Regal Building, gave way to The Cellar, Delhi's first ever discotheque that opened in March 1968. It was the brainchild of my brother-in-law and celebrated the young, the flower children who shared the sound and song of the Beatles and the Rolling Stones with their peers across the world. Our young generation came together regardless of cultural differences, language, caste or colour on the back of the music of the moment and the international dress code of blue jeans. A liberation of the spirit was happening and we were an intrinsic part of that psychedelic change. In contrast, Gaylord, with its Art Deco interiors, was a genteel restaurant in the same building where late morning 'parties', over tall, etched glasses of cold coffee and hot cups of cona coffee with chicken patties laced with chopped green chillies in vinegar, took place while checking out 'good' girls from 'good' families for eligible boys. The old and the new overlapped.

Further down, in the same building of which we were landlords, was Regal Cinema. It had a grand lobby with stairs leading up to the 'boxes' at the rear end of the hall. The pastel coloured walls along the sides were embellished with plaster of Paris statues painted white. It was quite spectacular in its heyday.

We would watch the noon show in the box with friends and lunch from The Cellar would be served to us during the screening. Those were the days! There were restaurants galore in Connaught Place and on adjoining streets. The city had a great culture of eating out, outside of the five-star hotels. Laguna, Alps, La Boheme, Volga, Chinese Room, Kwality, Kake da Hotel, Mikado, Standard and more. On the weekends, afternoon jam sessions, dancing to the beat of live jazz bands, would draw the young to the heart of the city. The patisserie of my time, Wenger's, is still there making the same delicious, incomparable chicken sandwiches, chocolate eclairs and lemon tarts.

I was a student at Modern School that sat amidst its sprawling grounds, just off Connaught Place, on Barakhamba Road. At the edge of the rear wall of its compound was one of Delhi's oldest markets—Bengali Market. It was and still is the best place in town to have chaat, gol guppas and to rendezvous with one's mates. It was also where we bought our school textbooks, compass sets and other stationery. To escape the monotony of a dull class, we would jump the wall and 'hang' at Nathu Ram's. And, we never got caught. Our teachers were special. Mr Menon, who taught us English, was the brother of Edadata Menon, editor of the *Patriot* newspaper, a left wing broadsheet. His home on campus was a safe refuge for us errant kids, because he understood our impatience and boredom and would spend time talking to us about 'men and matters' in the comfort of his living room with his wife feeding us cookies. The sanatorium was another place where we would admit ourselves as 'sick', having swallowed an aspirin with a Coca Cola to avoid the Sanskrit class. My favourite fellow student was Amjad Ali Khan who, like me, was bored to death doing maths and Sanskrit. We would chatter at the back of the classroom and failed consistently in mathematics. He was a child prodigy at the sarod, obsessed with music and nothing else. I, on the other hand, was a 'dilli-tante' in the making, interested in everything around me, wanting to do it all.

Sports were important in our school, as were other extracurricular activities. We had the famous painter couple, Kanval Krishna and his wife Devyani, teach us art in a splendid art room, outside which Tejbir and I would sneak happy moments together. We had a swimming pool, a hockey field, horses for those who wanted to learn to ride, a photography laboratory headed by O.P. Sharma, himself a professional photographer. Classical Indian dance, music and theatre were our other choices. Therefore, school was a blast. Our days were full, homework was marginal and rote learning was firmly discouraged. Sixty per cent marks and above was first division, fifty was second, forty was third and thirty-three per cent was the pass-mark. Seventy-five per cent in a subject was a distinction.

I loved the sports field. Athletics was very attractive for us girls because we could spend time on the tracks with the boys. And for me, swimming was a passion. I had learned in Bombay under the tutelage of Mrs

Anderson and had mastered the crawl style, whereas in Delhi, slow and boring breaststroke for the girls was the norm. I was the last swimmer in the relay because I was faster with freestyle and its vigorous ankle flapping. Conservative Delhi encouraged conservative swimsuits but I had come from Bombay and was, therefore, way out of line. The boys loved it. Shekhar Kapur, a senior in school, admired my 'ankles' and became a friend. Years later he cast me in *Masoom*, in a 'bit' role. The friendship has lasted all these decades.

School was a safe haven in the core of New Delhi. Tejbir and his friends would cycle to school from Golf Links through avenues that were virtually free of mad and crazy traffic. There was a politeness on the streets. Going to college was a different exercise altogether. Miranda House was miles away from home, and it would take me forty-five minutes in the bus to get to Delhi University, which was in Old Delhi near Civil Lines, the centre of the British government before the construction of the imperial capital was completed. Spread over a portion of the Ridge, Delhi University at the time housed some of the coveted colleges—Miranda House and St Stephen's being the most prestigious. At the end of the first year, I found myself expelled from Miranda House on rather flimsy grounds of not having attended the PT classes that were mandatory. A late riser, I could never make it from Chanakyapuri to Old Delhi by nine in the morning. And, more importantly, I was bored with that regimen.

I will never forget that day when I saw my name on a

form saying I had been expelled. Romila Thapar, the historian and also my aunt, lived with us. She was teaching at Delhi University and knew that I had been thrown out. I had to break the news to my parents and was fearful of how they would react. Romila came down to the garden with me where both my parents were, and I said to my father, 'Dad, I have been expelled from college', and his response was immediate. 'Congratulations, I was hoping one of my kids would be a rebel!' My mother was traumatized. Father then asked me what I would like to do. Would I like to do my A levels and try to get into Oxford University in England? It was his way of reassuring me that I was not daft or a failure.

For me, expulsion turned out to be a blessing in disguise. I joined the National School of Drama and did a three-year training course to become a theatre director. Situated on the roundabout of Mandi House and Bahawalpur House, in the vicinity of Bengali Market, with Connaught Place further afield, the NSD was a vibrant institution that produced some of India's finest actors and directors in film and theatre—Naseeruddin Shah, Om Puri, Raj Babbar, M.K. Raina, Surekha Sikri, Seema Biswas and more. Delhi staged and saw some of the best plays ever—*Medea*; the *Caucasian Chalk Circle* and *Three Penny Opera* written by Bertolt Brecht, translated into Hindi and directed by Carl Weber and Fritz Benewitz of the Berliner Ensemble; *Danton's Death* with an unforgettable performance by Naseer as Danton; *Jasma Odan*, the first ever rendering of a folk play in the Bhavai form behind a proscenium arch, translated from Gujarati into Hindi, with all the song and dance; *Tughlak*, unfolding against the backdrop of the Purana Qila, with Manohar Singh in the lead, capturing every nuance and inflection in his memorable performance; *Adhe Adhure*, on marital despair, with Surekha Sikri stealing the show; an adaptation of Anton Chekov's *Three Sisters*; *Godan* by Premchand, rechristened *Hori*, for which we students built a set to resemble a real village, out in the open, to inaugurate the Meghdoot Open Air Theatre. That was the first Hindi play I acted in with Manohar Singh in the lead, and me as his daughter-in-law, Jhuniya.

One memorable theatre experience I had outside of NSD was with Rajeev Sethi, who involved a whole bunch of us in a street theatre experiment. We enacted a play called *Mukhda Dekho Darpan Mein*, Look at your Face in the Mirror, which was about the bureaucracy and how it harasses the citizen instead of serving society. One performance was held at Vijay Chowk against the backdrop of North and South Blocks. Other shows took place in residential colonies where we would arrive in a truck, make a boxing ring kind of performance area and the residents would collect around us and we would perform. On one occasion we went out of town to Muzaffarnagar in Uttar Pradesh for a late night show on the outskirts of a village where we performed in front of an all-male audience.

The cultural centre of New Delhi in the sixties was spirited and lively, with exhibitions, theatre, music and dance, all happening around the Mandi House area. There was constant, active, professional theatre, the National School of Drama producing plays that set a new standard for the many amateur groups; regular art exhibitions showcased contemporary Indian painting and sculpture at Triveni Kala Sangam; Sumitra Charat Ram, the wife of the businessman Charat Ram, had set up Bharatiya Kala Kendra, a cultural and training institution that was created and supported by the Charat Ram family; the Kamani Auditorium was added by them to the landscape—it was one of the city's first well equipped theatres. This creative nerve centre was a lively adda that drew audiences for the many shows that were staged here in the evenings. The Lalit Kala and Sahitya and Sangeet Natak Akademis were housed in the same building as the NSD. Set up by the Government of India, these institutions were conceived to help nurture and enhance the cultural strengths of India. Sadly, like all our public sector initiatives, these once vibrant cultural spaces, too, have diluted into being sinecures for retired men and women who were once proponents of the arts. They need to be infused with new life and energy by populating them with new partners and fresh ideas.

In another part of town, alongside Lodhi Garden was the India International Centre, designed as a meeting place for ideas. It was wallowing in neglect and in the doldrums till C.D. Deshmukh the director, and his feisty wife, Durgabai who was his partner and most powerful influence, invited my father Romesh Thapar to inject the 'edifice' with some jaan, energy and activity. Designed by an expat architect, Joseph Stein, the building sat on land in an area that had been earmarked for 'institutions'. Just off South End Road, this was one of the first 'new' architectural experiments post Corbusier's work in Chandigarh. It was a stunning building that incorporated both Indian motifs and a modern look and feel in terms of scale and materials used. Very quickly, the IIC became an active and celebrated intellectual and cultural centre of New Delhi.

There were lectures every evening, exhibitions, film shows and music recitals, seminars and conferences. The library was given a fresh lease of life under the able administration of Mr Wajid and his capable lieutenant, Mr Kaul, who eventually took charge when Wajid Sahib retreated to Kashmir. Fresh, unexposed talent congregated here, young and old, with ideas to share, and those wanting to see and hear, look and listen, came to experience a new, vibrant energy. The lounge and dining hall were rocking with friends and new acquaintances. Old-fashioned 'clubs' had become passé for the happening crowd, and were acceptable only to the very young at one end of the spectrum and the fuddy-duddy at the other end. Delhi was changing yet again. The city was growing up.

÷

In the 1980s, especially after it hosted the Asian Games in 1982, and there were reports of huge sums of money being made on construction contracts and infrastructure projects, the city underwent a transformation unlike anything it had ever seen in the preceding decades, some of it good, some of it bad. It would also in the course of the next few decades become the undisputed No 1 City in the country firmly elbowing aside the claims of rival contenders like Bombay, Calcutta and Madras. We will examine all this and more in the chapter, 'New New Delhi', but before that we get there it is necessary to get beneath the skin of the 'capital city' in the next chapter.

CAPITAL CITY

When Pandit Jawaharlal Nehru presided over the treasury benches in Parliament, from 1947 to 1964, a sense of hope pervaded the capital and its inhabitants, and I'm being more literal than not, because we so wanted to believe in him and all those first builders of modern India. There was an excitement that was infectious even for young impressionable teenagers like myself. Panditji embraced the world. The gates of his residence, Teen Murti House, were always open and people flowed in and ideas flowed out. He was, in a word, accessible. One example of this openness remains firmly etched in my memory, when the 'voice' of my father, who 'spoke' commentaries for Films Division documentaries, was banned, by Shri Keskar who was in charge of the Ministry of Information and Broadcasting. The reason—Romesh Thapar is a communist! Doing these voice-overs had brought in a regular income for our small nuclear family when we were living in Bombay. The ban was a blow. A friend of my father's suggested he go to Delhi and meet Nehru. Astounded by the suggestion, Father brushed the idea aside but was persuaded to send a letter to the prime minister to ask how and why the authorities believed that a 'voice' could be politically insidious. Within twelve hours, Nehru had telephoned Keskar and the ban was lifted. But, in true babu style, his name was 'censored' from the credit roll. It read: 'Voice . . .'! The difference today is that the PMO would have asked the Information and Broadcasting Ministry, through their 'snail daak', or internal mail, to constitute a GoM and the problem would fester and become malignant.

Nehru had strong views on every conceivable subject, was hugely well read, interested, engaged, energetic, judgmental, vocal and committed to the people of India in a real, tactile way. India and its dignity was his first priority. He had a forthright vision for this nation and its relations with the region and the world. For us children, Chacha Nehru was an enigma, a hero and a mentor whom we respected and looked to for inspiration. The rose he wore in the lapel of his jacket and the pandas he housed in his large garden, were symbols of his profound love of nature and commitment to her conservation and health. I recall a memorable moment when we had sneaked into Teen Murti House and peeked through the keyhole of his study, thrilled to see the prime minister reading at his desk. He came out in a while and asked to be photographed with us, not the other way round. That was the stark difference between then and now. Faith and trust, graciousness and good manners were the norm.

The prime minister would be driven around in his

own Ambassador car, much like any ordinary citizen, except that he would have a single outrider on a motorcycle leading the way. There was no lal batti or absurd heralding or announcing of his presence like they do now. He visited friends in the city for dinner, smoked a cigarette when he felt like it without the hypocrisy of smoking behind closed doors. There were no false hang-ups then, like those that have saturated the political scene today. Here was the first prime minister of liberated India who rode a horse, loved the Himalaya, and all mountains, where he would ride and trek. He loved the Kashmir valley. Dachigam, the forest on the outskirts of Srinagar, was his favourite retreat, his island for contemplation. He enjoyed the company of intellectuals and philosophers, historians and writers. He reached out to ordinary Indians, citizens of the Republic. Meeting them was a priority for him. He had time for children and their curiosity. Culture, in all its manifestations, was saluted, absorbed and given its rightful importance. There was only one vote bank for him. It was India. Over sixty years on, the prime minister remains trapped in an ivory tower, silent and disconnected. He neither walks the nation, nor talks to it.

Nehru invited Roberto Rossellini who was, at the time, married to Ingrid Bergman, to make a film on India. Rossellini did come, and left this country with the woman he fell in love with during his sojourn here, Sonali Dasgupta. Sonali was married to Hari Dasgupta who was working with Rossellini as an assistant director.

Hari persuaded Roberto to hire Sonali as his secretary
and the rest is history. One New Year's Eve, at my
parents' traditional party, Sonali, shy, gorgeous and
tall, with her open hair flowing down to her waist,
danced with Roberto and into one of his longest
partnerships that took her away from home and from
her first child whom she met decades later. When Hari
protested and tried to stop her from leaving, it was
Nehru who cleared her passport and one for her infant
son, had them facilitated and out on a flight to Paris,
where she lived incognito in Cartier Bresson's studio
until Ingrid agreed to 'free' Roberto.

Nehru gave Le Corbusier (or Charles-Édouard
Jeanneret-Gris) the opportunity to build a city. Prem
Thapar, another brother of my grandfather's, was a
secretary in the Indian Civil Service and attached to Le
Corbusier through that period. A large expanse of land
was earmarked for this new, contemporary city. Corbu,
as Le Corbusier was referred to, had been given a clean
slate to showcase his grand intellectual and architectural
genius. Chandigarh rose out of the dust, at the foot of
the Simla Hills, its dramatic, concrete sculptural
government buildings making a statement of modernity;
the simple lines with primary colours adding a dimension
to the cold and sterile texture of the concrete he used. A
superimposed, inorganic 'city' was forced upon the
landscape. It was in sharp contrast to the New Delhi
built by Edwin Lutyens.

Nehru connected India and the world. He believed in
grand partnerships and engagements. He encouraged

and endorsed them. I recall it being a very heady moment for my parents too, who belonged to the generation that was caught up with the responsibility of building the new nation state. *Seminar* reflected those years with much candour. It was one of the forums for free debate and has survived and grown over fifty-four years.

It was a time when Delhi as the intellectual capital of India was beginning to take root. Nehru encouraged young economists and academics to participate in seminars, discussions and interactions with the political class. The bureaucrats too, were men and women of great erudition. B.K. Nehru, L.K. Jha, L.P. Singh, P.N. Haksar to name just a few, were non-partisan secretaries to the Government of India. One never saw the exalted babus of those days at impersonal and mindless cocktail parties or corporate dinners. They were by and large anonymous and powerful as advisors and implementers of policy. They met the best and brightest at small get-togethers. They listened and responded. They engaged with serious intent. The 'steel frame' had not yet begun to corrode.

Criticism did not deter leaders from meeting those men and women, journalists and editors, who questioned them and their actions. There was a maturity that tolerated dissent. To 'sulk' because a supporter had disagreed with you, was definitely not the norm. Leaders were confident. They walked the talk, in the real sense, unlike today when politicians 'walk the talk' on television for half-an-hour and then retreat into the safe custody of sycophants.

How Delhi has changed from Dilli. Its rulers of today are obsessed with isolating themselves, caged into their homes, offices and cars, surrounded by gun-toting police and security guards, defying the fundamental tenets of a liberal democracy and all its processes, ignoring the mechanisms of engagement with the very people who elect them to power. It is through such behaviour that they have lost the great head-start India had in the early decades after Independence.

+

During the height of Hindi-Chini bhai bhai, as very, very young kids, we too believed that China and India were inseparable. Then, in October 1962, the Chinese attacked our frontiers at Se La and Nathu La. My grandfather's younger brother was, at the time, Chief of Staff of the Indian Army. Nehru and Krishna Menon were in denial and had been refusing to take note of the signs that pointed to a changing China that the army had been trying to bring to their attention for some time. Shattered, Nehru went into a depression and passed away on 27 May 1964, a broken man. We all wept. Young and old, the spontaneous outpouring of grief from the gut, immersed Delhi in tears. I have never seen a procession like the one to pay homage to Nehru—ever. Everyone came out and lined the streets. Rich, poor and migrant, India was one that day— Nehru's India. Speaking the commentary from the roof of a building on the Ring Road, as the cortege moved towards Shantivan, forest of peace, I heard my father's voice break down into controlled sobs, as he paid his tribute to an extraordinary man. We had gone past another milestone.

The chattering classes, propelled by the lazy amongst the peripheral politicians, assumed Indira Gandhi would inherit her father's mantle. They were jolted out of their rather slapdash assessment when Lal Bahadur Shastri became India's second prime minister. The capital felt different. The energy, the myriad interests and intellectual 'bounce' of Jawaharlal Nehru that had charged its atmosphere was missing. The political mood in Delhi became low-key—difficult to describe. My memory of that time is the dominating presence of L.K. Jha who was Shashtriji's right hand man. Unusually tall and handsome, Jha had a sharp intellect, huge knowledge and was very well spoken. He had the ability to embrace young and old and treated all at par.

There was much talk in the early sixties that India needed to exit the command economy and 'restructure' to compete with the world using her enormous skills and human resource. L.K. Jha tried to get that process going but his efforts were in vain. Then, in early August of 1965, war broke out between India and Pakistan. Initially combat was on land but later, on 1 September, air attacks began. India gained territory on the Western Front in the Lahore and Sialkot sectors and Pakistan in the Kutch sector. The battle was intense involving armoured corps and infantry on both sides as well as naval interventions. At the end of September that same year there was a ceasefire and in January 1966 both

countries signed a peace agreement in Tashkent. But
sadly, matters got hugely complicated when Prime
Minister Lal Bahadur Shastri who had just signed off
on the deal, died suddenly, at 2.15 a.m. Indian Standard
Time, in Tashkent, cutting short his term in office. I
remember his body being brought back to India on a
special aircraft, with Pakistan's General Ayub Khan as
one of his pallbearers.

In the dead of night, having had confirmed intimation
about Shastri's demise, the Congress Party leadership
began to work on projecting his successor. It was my
first ever bird's-eye view of political maneuvering behind
the scenes. The heavyweight oldies in the Party, wily
and ambitious, had thrown themselves behind the
conservative strongman Morarji Desai, and had begun
to queue up outside his home from the early hours of
the morning. Indira Gandhi was Minister for
Information and Broadcasting in Shastri's cabinet at
the time. She was young, she was a woman, she was the
daughter of Nehru. Her credentials were perfect for
anyone who represented a youthful and aspiring India
at the time, but the 'syndicate', the bastion of the aged
in the Congress Party, were clear that they did not want
her at the helm. She was more left of centre. The
Opposition too, much like today, abused her by calling
her a 'gungi gudiya', demeaning her personally. Ram
Manohar Lohia, a socialist leader of the time, had
coined the phrase. Believing that they had nothing to
lose, a group of Indira Gandhi's close supporters—
Dinesh Singh, Inder Gujral, Romesh Thapar amongst

others—decided to jump into the fray and lobby hard
for her candidature. Within forty-eight hours, the queues
of Congressmen, with bowed heads and folded hands,
were winding their way to 1 Safdarjung Road, her
home. Congresswomen, and women at large, sensing
that she might win, were overwhelmed by what that
might portend in terms of gender acceptability and
freedom.

At some point in the evening, before her name was
officially announced, my father came home and said to
us, 'We have won, Indira will be the prime minister'.
Stunned with disbelief and much joy, my mother, my
aunt Romila Thapar, and I demolished a bottle of
Slivovitz, an East European schnapps, in wild celebration
of 'young, contemporary, female power'. The 'gungi
gudiya' had showed her paces, and would go on to
become the most powerful prime minister India has
ever had.

Delhi was buzzing again. We had a woman at the
helm, one who wore the most wonderful handloom
saris and looked so elegant in them. She had become a
style icon for the contemporary Indian woman. Till
that moment, I had been told by the trendy amongst
my friends that I dressed like an ayah in my handloom
saris. One fine morning, I was leading the tribe with my
collection. 'Made in India' started to become a brand.
Pride in things Indian began to permeate into the lives
of the last of the Br-indians and their 'haw-haw' clones!

Pupul Jayakar was handed the responsibility of
restoring and reinventing the great handloom past of

this country by secretary to the Government of India, T.T. Krishnamachari. I remember Pupul telling me that when she was offered the task to reinvent the handloom sector, she had not even seen a loom. Then began a voyage of discovery. She travelled around the country, visited the famed weaving centres of India, from Kerala up the coast and inland to Bihar and the Northeast, looking and listening, delving into information that existed either in fabric fragments or in memory and word of mouth. She then steadily began the process of restoration. She had the tacit backing of the then government and was able to establish a chain of Weavers Service Centres across the country to rejuvenate dying weaving skills and traditions. She put handlooms on the map once again and became the uncrowned cultural Tsarina of India till the end of the Indira Gandhi era.

On the other side, digging deep into the vast treasure trove of handicrafts, Kamaladevi Chattopadhyay established Naika in Mehrauli, and travelled through the subcontinent, into remote and isolated areas where no-one had dared to venture, to identify and collect the most extraordinary objects of everyday use, crafted and patterned with a delicacy and sensibility that remains unmatched. It was Rajeev Sethi who took the baton from her and moved on. The work of both these grand women was finally showcased for the larger international world in the eighties through the Festivals of India held in the United States of America, Britain and Europe. These two remarkable women rejuvenated the latent designer in all of us. The world was stunned by the fragile beauty of the living skills of India's artisans.

Pupul Jayakar, Kamaladeviji, Prem Bery, Sina Kaul, Mrs Vir Singh were all committed to the great skill of the hands, the indigenous 'information technology', passed down through generations, that was the legacy of the people of this rich subcontinent. They respected the people of India and endeavoured to incorporate their diverse strengths and skills into the mainstream of economic activity and growth. They wore handloom saris, tribal necklaces and silver bracelets and led the 'fashion trend' by example.

There were other extraordinary women who bestrode the domain of Delhi, setting the standards and trends. Padmaja Naidu, daughter of Sarojini, lived in an outhouse behind the rear garden of Teen Murti House and was the chairperson of the Nehru Memorial Trust. She was the quintessential woman, strong and feminine, opinionated and compassionate, with unwavering values and ethics. Those were the 'jewels' that we treasured. She sat on an imposing throne-like chair every evening with her foot poised on a footstool, dressed in a resplendent sari with a flower in her hair, and greeted a wide cross section of visitors who engaged with her, sharing ideas, indulging in heated discussions and arguments.

÷

Like her father before her, Indira Gandhi had a sense of history and posterity. I recall her inviting Buckminster

Fuller to India. He was a legend of our times, and she had asked him to work up a plan wherein he would use the geodesic dome that he had invented and created, to radically re-design the airport in Delhi. Imagine having to merely add another dome as air traffic increased and required more space, with no change in the exterior design. The idea was streets ahead of its time, particularly today, when all airports in the world look the same and need constant additions to the main frame. She organized a dinner where Bucky Fuller and J. Krishnamurti had an unending 'conversation', both speaking a 'language' that neither really comprehended. She could think out of the box. She enjoyed new encounters.

The gates of 1 Safdarjung Road were always open, Indira Gandhi had friends over to dinner, she went out to dinner, went shopping, was seen around the city. Despite being a shy and private person, she engaged with Delhi. She did not cringe with fear and isolate herself from her people.

Indira Gandhi lived opposite the Delhi Gymkhana Club. As teenagers, we would spend hours at the club—play tennis, use the library and swim. Sitting out on the lawns we would devour chicken sandwiches, dipping them in ketchup, drinking a ghastly, aerated cola called Vimto. Often, when driving out of the club gates we would see Indira Gandhi entering her home in an Ambassador car that did not have a red light on its roof. She did not need to show off her status with a noisy, intrusive siren or flashing lights and ill-mannered escort cars. She exuded power because of how she ruled and connected with her people. We were confident and proud as well, because the leadership was setting new standards of confidence and pride.

During this period, as Indira Gandhi was gradually but surely ascending the power ladder, a mysterious political scandal hit the news. An 'Indira-like' slightly high-pitched 'voice', had rung up a bank manager claiming she was the prime minister and asking for the release of a large chunk of money. The money was allegedly released and it was believed at the time that it was used to fund the Mukti Bahini, a 'citizens' brigade' that was ostensibly working to overthrow the Pakistani state of East Pakistan, and declare independence under the leadership of Mujibur Rahman. As the story, which seemed very far-fetched, was exposed and unravelled, many players in this bizarre scandal began to die accidentally or in unimaginable circumstances. It is now remembered as the Nagarwala Case. It was scary at the time and conjured up all manner of images that spelt conspiracy and volatile, unpredictable rajniti. Finally, our military victory, on the eastern border, and the surrender of 100,000 Pakistani troops at the time of 'the liberation of East Pakistan' and the founding of Bangladesh, established Indira Gandhi as the Queen Empress of India, in fact, of the subcontinent. There was an euphoria, laced with jingoism, that flooded Delhi for a while after which the city settled down and normal, ordinary activity resumed.

÷

It was in the seventies that things really began to change. First, there was the war of course. And then, the dreaded word, 'corruption', began to enter our conversation, began to attach itself to politicians and people in political life. As the old guard began to retire, and a generational shift began to take place, along with it came a new more venal morality that we could scarcely comprehend, let alone adjust to.

Politics, too, was becoming more volatile. Extra-constitutional interference in processes of governance was permitted; it began to anger some but gave others the signal that if they became unquestioning foot soldiers, they could benefit. As stories of nepotism and illegalities spread, the politics of the city took on dangerously potent dark and charcoal hues. It was sometime in 1974 that L.N. Mishra, a member of the inner core of the Congress Party, was blown to smithereens by a bomb that blasted through the Samastipur railway station in Bihar. It was alleged that he masterminded the 'dirty tricks department' of the Party at the time. Mishra's death was a precursor of things to come. Indira Gandhi, once relaxed and open, now an increasingly insecure and paranoid leader, declared an ill-advised state of internal Emergency on 25 June 1975. The liberal and democratic march forward, carefully crafted by our founding fathers, by Gandhiji and Jawaharlal Nehru, had been rudely diverted from its course.

Confidence and pride was replaced by fear and anger. Our rights had been snatched from us, the jewels of our great legacy and tradition had been temporarily stolen. Delhi was the epicentre of this quake. We were compelled to alter the movement of our lives, but our minds and souls remained acute and sharp within our artificial cages. The great middle class ceased to speak out, fell in line and was silent. In the countryside, the concerns were roti, kapda aur makaan, not political jockeying for power. The small intellectual elite spoke out despite censorship and fought the imposed 'change'. My parents had opposed the Emergency publicly and vocally despite having been politically close to Indira Gandhi till then. A tension, the like of which Delhi had not experienced for decades, had begun to suffocate the city and its citizens.

I had never been in a situation that demanded that you cease to think and speak, debate and argue, agree to disagree. Freedom was my birthright, or so I had been told by my heroes, by Gandhiji and Panditji, by my parents and theirs. Now we were being told to suppress what we felt strongly about and thought was wrong. It was a bizarre contortion, unfathomable and upsetting because it disturbed the idea of India we had believed in. When we protested it was usually against wrong and illegal acts that were taking place around us, but then we always felt we could access elected representatives to put the correctives in place. The neta and the babu were parallel lines of power. The elected leaders called the shots and the babus implemented the orders. That had changed.

My parents had an 'open house' on New Year's Eve

that had, over the decades, become an unbroken tradition. A minimum of five hundred people, young and old, would come and go, drink a special formula rum punch, and eat home-made kebabs and other delectable goodies that my mother would conjure up, and we would all have a blast dancing to the music of the fifties and sixties. We would paint satirical political slogans that summed up the year gone by on posters that would be pasted on the walls and doors inside our home. The guest-list, if you could call it that, was eclectic—politicians and painters, writers and administrators, servicemen and women and academics, students and musicians, dancers and singers, a group that represented India, a multi-faceted urban India with its many dimensions and layers. It was 'open' in the true sense of the word, and always attracted diversity and contradictions.

On 31 December 1975, my father, greatly depressed, turned off the lights and closed the gate. Only close family and friends came to dinner and sat about chatting, sharing stories that came by word of mouth from across the northern states where the effects of the Emergency were making an impact. Our friends in government and politics were too scared to be seen at our home throughout that period lest they be marked as dissenters.

During those years, Sanjay Gandhi, the younger son of Indira Gandhi, was the de facto centre of power with his group of aspiring loyalists, operating from his mother's home. He rode roughshod over all procedure forcing Congress politicians and the bureaucrats, both custodians of the Constitution of India, to fall in line and follow his directives. Some did so out of sheer fear and others fell in line because of the lucrative sinecures out of the young man was able to grant them. Sanjay had a five-point programme for India, that sounded fine, but he implemented that plan like a dictator, rather than through the processes of democracy and the laws of the land. One of the points was 'family planning', something that was imperative for a country like India where a population explosion was underway. But the sad truth was that his processes of forcible vasectomy across north India was an inhumane, ruthless assault that set back the family planning programme by decades. That one programme let loose during the Emergency, lost the Congress its election. It is alleged that many were victimized and threatened if they opposed the 'leader'. Others were severely punished. Some were brutalized.

On 31 December 1976, after nearly two years of despair and despondency, we realized something momentous was about to happen. Again, we had a small gathering at home when suddenly, at about eleven at night, the doorbell rang and in walked P.N. Dhar, who was secretary to Indira Gandhi and a close family friend who had stayed away from us from 25 June 1975 onwards. With him and his wife came Dr Karan Singh, another close friend who had kept his distance as well. They had shunned us on New Year's Eve the previous year and we were surprised by this intrusion.

My father, however, did not miss a beat and in his loud, booming voice said, 'Indira must have decided to call elections'. She had taken the decision. The fear of her coterie to engage with us had lifted. Even they, the most powerful, could breathe freely once again, and renew dropped friendships. We brought in my father's birthday at midnight with hope and relief in the belief that 'liberation' from the Emergency was within reach.

It had been a very treacherous period in Delhi and India's contemporary history. With the announcement of the Emergency at midnight on 25 June 1975, all the stalwart leaders of the opposition parties of India had been arrested in a pre-dawn swoop. It was horrific. Without cause, our tallest leaders in this democracy were imprisoned. The city too was assaulted. Turkman Gate, one of the many that led into the walled city of Shahjahanabad and where the descendants of Mughal India lived, was demolished by bulldozers, its inhabitants flung into ghettos across the river Jamuna, on to its flood plain. Homeless and amputated from their traditional vocations, a section of Dilliwallahs were impoverished for all time to come. Nothing has changed for them over the decades that followed.

During the months that the Emergency was in play, ruling our external and private lives, new friends came forward, united by a common cause, to work to restore the freedoms that were guaranteed by our Constitution. Many were odd bedfellows who drifted away once elections were announced, but some remained. One of those was Piloo Mody and his wife, Vina. Piloo had been taken into custody in the pre-dawn arrests on 26 June 1975. A large, overweight man and a gourmand with a sharp intellect and a great sense of humour, he was horrified to discover, when he arrived in jail, that there was no Western-style potty. He sent a message to Indira Gandhi saying so and the same evening, she ordered a brick platform to be constructed around the squat-type, for his comfort. It was one of the quirks of her personality that, despite having sent them to jail, she was accessible to her political opponents. Vina would take the dogs to visit Piloo in jail, much to the chagrin of the jailers who could not eavesdrop on their conversation because they were scared silly by the horse-like hounds.

Many years before, Piloo, an active member of the Swatantra Party, published a tabloid called *March of the Nation*. One morning my father found it had published a mischievous and utterly false story on its front page, suggesting that my father, Renu Chakravarty and the personal physician of Nehru were planning to poison the prime minister. It was unbelievable and wholly fictitious, made up in the imagination of some devious and sick reporter. Father sent an immediate legal notice to the entire family that owned the paper, Sir Homi Mody included. There was a full-page apology on the front page of the next edition. The relationship between my parents and the Modys was distant to say the least, they were ideologically opposed to one another, and this incident made it cold and frigid. However, when Piloo along with other major leaders of the

Opposition were arrested on that fateful 'Emergency' morning, all liberal-minded individuals came together in solidarity. Through the Emergency and after it had been lifted, Piloo, Vina and our family became close again and regulars at each other's homes. Piloo was wonderful, warm and welcoming. He was a fund of stories, political and others, and entranced us with his storytelling skills. Dinner at the Modys was always a treat with a prawn curry that no other has been able to match. He was a backbencher in Parliament and always brought on the laughs. He was a landmark in Delhi and I was enveloped by a profound sadness the day he died. I had lost a friend and father figure. Our ideological differences had never figured in our affectionate relationship.

When Indira Gandhi announced elections, there was one extraordinary and large public election rally in the city in 1977 that I attended and will never forget. It happened on Rajpath and it was jam-packed with ordinary people who jostled each other as they fought to grab a small space on the grass and tarmac for themselves, all the way from Vijay Chowk to India Gate, waiting to hear leaders of the then Opposition speak. Vijaya Lakshmi Pandit, Jawaharlal Nehru's much-loved sister and aunt of Indira Gandhi, was on the stage with the others and then, suddenly, a senior minister and Congressman, Jagjivan Ram, a powerful and influential Harijan leader, joined them. A deafening cheer broke out that bounced off the skies. He had decided to speak out against the constrictive Emergency.

My mother, sitting with me in the crowd, whispered: 'It's like the mood at the time of Quit India'. Indians had united against repression and anti-Constitutional acts.

This may well have been the moment when Indira Gandhi recognized the reality on the ground, the palpable truth—that her countrymen were desperate to break free from the oppression she had unleashed upon them. She retreated within herself, aware that she could well lose the forthcoming election if the mood at this rally was anything to go by.

Yet, the democrat in her, led Indira Gandhi to declare elections and go back to the people for their verdict, against much advice not to do so. Delhi came alive again. People were talking, debating and the pent-up frustration and fear of many months, poured out in the living rooms, in the coffee houses and on to the ever alive streets. Delhi was dancing again, waiting to vote, as was the rest of India. North India voted her and her party out of office with a devastating mandate. South India, unaffected by the assaults of the Emergency, supported the Congress Party. The numbers were inadequate to make government. No single party had a majority.

Watching the results coming in, we knew the Emergency, and the Congress Party and its prime mover, Indira, who were behind it, had been rejected by the people of India. But the fear and lies that had enveloped us all, had not evaporated. My father had a call that morning from someone high up in the secretariat, who warned that the counting might yet be called off since the defeat was a real possibility, and that both Ma and Dad should move out of the house in case there was a another sweep of arrests. Insecurity and fear of the possible consequences of losing power had entered the mindset and personas of the ruling regime.

My parents called us, told us not to be concerned about their safety and said they would come to our home in Sujan Singh Park as soon as the results were officially announced. Armed with egg sandwiches and a flask of coffee, they drove around Delhi and appeared at our door at seven in the evening, relieved and elated. 'They have lost by huge leads that cannot be fudged,' said my father. It was time for a strong and delicious whisky. Friends began to pour in and we had the best ever party, with people sitting on the stairways of the building and in every conceivable space they could find. Even Akbar Ahmed, close associate and friend of Sanjay Gandhi came, ostensibly to mourn the defeat of his friends and to imbibe some strong brew. It was a bring-a-bottle-and-a-laugh party, without an 'invitation card'.

On the streets of Delhi there was instinctive, wild celebration. The men and women who were the faces of Mrs Gandhi's repressive regime lost by unimaginable margins and the streets filled with people from all walks of life, bursting into song, dance and laughter. The dil of Dilli was free again. The city centre that night was Bahadur Shah Zafar Marg, named after the last Mughal who ruled from Delhi, where many newspaper offices are housed, and where large boards showed the incoming results. Loud cries of happiness resounded when Bansi Lal, the strongman of Haryana and Sanjay Gandhi's henchman, lost. Ice-cream vendors distributed free chocobars to everyone around in mad, uncontrollable joy. Delhi was alive that night, competing with life and action in Jama Masjid and Chandni Chowk. An ancient aunt of my father's, with a bunch of equally old biddies, hired a taxi late at night to go from Hauz Khaz to Bahadur Shah Zafar Marg to watch the results. The mood was unforgettable.

÷

A motley group of aspiring leaders and parties, all of whom had been against the Emergency, came to power. Although they shared no common ground politically or economically, they tried to make a go of it, on the basis of their opposition to the Emergency but as that no longer existed the Janata Party, as the coalition was called, was a government with neither purpose nor energy and it soon collapsed under the weight of its own contradictions. The country refused to tolerate, for long, the petty politicking, the corrupt and inappropriate practices of governance and the tireless jousting for power that the leaders of the Janata Party indulged in. The same men and women who had damned the system now merrily adopted it without compunction. Corruption found a fertile breeding ground, and grew unchecked. Governance took a rear seat allowing personal and greed-laden agendas to dominate. I believe this was the watershed period when India moved into the phase where corruption became an entrenched part of politics. Unfortunately, the country has been unable to rid itself of that malignant virus.

Justice Shah was appointed to head a commission of inquiry mandated to look into the malpractices that had made the Emergency the horror it was. Tejbir and I must have attended every hearing in that open court, learning, by listening to hours of interrogation, how politicians and bureaucrats misused and misinterpreted the rules and norms to circumvent processes, mechanisms and delivery systems. Their blatant arrogance was being exposed in full view of the public. Political and administrative scandal upon scandal were unearthed and exposed.

A politically savvy Indira Gandhi was watching this moral, political and administrative unravelling of the 'alternate collective' from her temporary home on Willingdon Crescent, now Mother Teresa Crescent, and very quickly began to conceive a strategy and prepare for her return. When mid-term elections were called, Indira Gandhi, well poised with her legendary passion and energy, led her battered and tattered party to a spectacular comeback and victory. She moved back into 1 Safdarjung Road.

However, this time round, a profound sense of insecurity had set in. No one was trusted. Coteries developed. Favourites ruled the roost, disabling all internal dissent and deliberations. The 'truth' of what was going on out there never got to her. Barriers, both tangible and intangible, came up and barricaded ideas and free flowing information. Indira began to be isolated from dissenting views and her small band of lieutenants, led by her younger son Sanjay, seeing an opportunity to protect their own interests, and deflect attention away from their insubstantial intellectual and professional qualifications and other inadequacies, 'shielded' her and cut her off deliberately from the open, liberal space that had been her hallmark and strength in her previous avatar, that which had nurtured her and given her the confidence that she exuded.

Delhi too, changed. It had become restrictive and suspicious. Open gates to homes and offices were gradually closing and the gatekeepers, our chowkidars, who were much like members of the larger family, were replaced by impersonal guards, callous, curt and unpleasant, who couldn't care less about graceful, polite behaviour. Politicians and bureaucrats began to see themselves as God's own selected few, isolating themselves from the city and its people. An arrogance of authority had seeped into our domain. Our city, Delhi, had rejected us and become the home and 'capital' of the politician and the babu at the cost of Dilliwallahs.

÷

Throughout the seventies and the early eighties the city underwent its first transformation from the sunny, open capital that I had come to as a young girl, grown up in, and married into. Now, in Indira Gandhi's second stint as prime minister, in the darker more corrupt regime

105

that she presided over, money began to speak, and a
new breed of land developer and contractor began to
alter the contours of the city. Unauthorized construction,
haphazard planning, sprawling townships and
residential developments mushroomed for miles in every
direction. Fortunes were made by unscrupulous
developers and ministers. And every day more and
more people poured into the city, because suddenly,
overnight it seemed, Delhi was beginning to be where
the action was, even though it would be another decade
before the economic liberalization was ushered in by
Prime Minister Narasimha Rao and his Finance Minister
Manmohan Singh after the country went almost
bankrupt.

106   But I'm getting ahead of my story. Before the new
dawn of the nineties we would have to experience the
darkness of the eighties beginning with the death of the
prime minister's son Sanjay in 1980 in a plane crash.
Although her older son Rajiv stepped up, Indira never
quite recovered her nerve and composure or regained
her inner strength, and all her subsequent actions in
one way or another seemed to be marked by the loss
she had suffered. Four years later, the city hit rock
bottom. Indira was shot dead by her security guards in
retaliation for the storming of the Golden Temple, by
the Indian army on 6 June 1984, in a desperate effort to
capture Sant Bhindranwale, who had challenged the
state and who many believed was the 'creation' of the
Congress Party in an attempt to play power politics in
Punjab.

As soon as she was killed, thousands of innocent Sikhs were brutally massacred by armed thugs often led by politicians belonging to the Congress party.

Dilli had changed forever. A dreadful polarization between communities that were, till recently, considered to be the same, had been planted in the soil of this ancient city.

My husband is Sikh and we, as a family, felt the tremors of alienation. The family of the man who had built New Delhi, Sir Sobha Singh, was taken by my parents to their home on Kautilya Marg. My parents were Hindus by birth, but living atheists, and chances were that their home would be safe from the marauding bands of lumpen gangsters who had taken charge of our public spaces. It was a free-for-all with the administration having failed to abide by its mandate.

During this awful period, there were occasions when conversations would stop when Tejbir and I entered a friend's house for dinner, lest we as Sikhs, betrayed confidences or carried tales. Trust amongst friends had broken down. Peculiar comments had to be ignored if only to keep the peace. Sikhs couldn't be trusted any more, was one refrain I had to hear and file away in the inner recesses of my mind. At one dinner, a senior member of the foreign service, a Muslim by faith, pompously announced that we Sikhs needed to be taught a lesson; that Muslims had been treated like 'second-class citizens' and we needed to be put through a similar trajectory. We were horrified and left the room. The wounds were raw and painful and we did

107

not deserve to be at the receiving end of such appalling comments by a senior government functionary. New relationships were born, many were written off for all time. A strange, rather perverse cleansing was underway. The city of my carefree and younger years had been put through the wringer and was becoming unrecognizable, losing its tactile energy and strength.

+

Rajiv Gandhi came to power at a time when India was looking for radical change and for a break with the corroded and tortured past. He was young, had a very attractive wife and two delightful children. He embodied the straightforwardness that a young India, enterprising and raring to go but till then restrained, was looking forward to. He reached out to young Indians, spoke their language, engaged with them and set fresh standards, exuding a profound sense of hope. He was far more inclusive in his style of governance than the regimes before him. Many younger politicians entered the fray and got to prominent positions. Professionals from outside of politics, from the corporate world and from academia, technocrats and scientists, were brought in to create new strategies and plans for modernizing the nation. Amongst them was Sam Pitroda, who having set up C-DOT, the forerunner to direct long distance dialling that connected village India to the mandi and more, was mandated to craft technology missions for essential civil services ranging from water to education. His pioneering work remains valid today as does his energetic, unfailing optimism. Rajiv brought technological tools into the offices of government and encouraged a move to modernity of mechanisms and processes of governance. Then suddenly one day, an unsubstantiated scandal pierced through the walls of the city that shook the foundations of the Rajiv Gandhi government—alleged kickbacks on the Bofors gun deal. Till date and despite the BJP government having been in power from the end of the last century into the early years of this one, no one has been able to nail Rajiv Gandhi and his family on the Bofors Scandal, but it debilitated his government and punctured the prevailing euphoria that political and administrative change was imminent.

I often wonder whether the unsubstantiated 'exposure' was a deliberate ploy by vested interest groups, to try and discredit a clean, intelligent and honest politician who could well have cleansed a festering, dirty system of politics that protected the corrupt, in both the political and the administrative class. Had Rajiv been free to deliver what he had set out to, India would not have lost two precious decades wallowing in corruption, led by self-serving politicians and babus who have strangled the vitality of this young nation over the last three decades. Had he been able to make his dream into a tangible reality, India would have been a different country as it headed deeper into the twenty-first century.

After the meaningless killing of Rajiv Gandhi, his widow retreated into herself and spent many years alone, grappling with her intense grief and teaching herself about the India that Nehru, and those who followed him to the gaddi, had built. She is today one of India's most astute and dignified leaders, never speaks out of turn and has become an enigma. Her critics are more often than not men and women now on the periphery of power politics, who were once, in her carefree days, Sonia's 'pals'. Many chip away at her, criticizing her every move and utterance, only because they feel slighted and cut off.

In 2004, she single-handedly, resurrected a sleeping but divided Congress Party, became its glue, led it from the front, silently fighting the abuse hurled at her, and succeeded in putting the UPA coalition in place, which although disparate, has stayed in office for a decade. She initiated some of the most progressive acts that were voted upon in India's Parliament and established as law, better, more transparent, democratic and inclusive instruments of governance for the next phase of politics in India. Right to Information was one such salutary intervention, a game changer, as were some others. She brought the marginalized into the frame of incentives and growth, creating some checks and balances that stalled crony capitalism from invading and battering every inch of India. Both Rajiv and Sonia, in their respective reigns, worked at changing the course of the country, adding value to the vision of the founding fathers, infusing the larger domain of India with new ideas and initiatives.

THE NEW NEW DELHI

Nobody expected much of wily old Prime Minister P.V. Narasimha Rao and his rather well regarded Finance Minister, Manmohan Singh. Everyone knew Rao was a faithful retainer of the Gandhi-Nehru clan, and a crafty political survivor, but few expected him to throw off the shackles on the economy in the manner he did, and give Manmohan Singh the freedom to craft an economic policy that would finally give the nation's entrepreneurial spirit a chance to flourish. However, India was in a terrible financial mess when the IMF loan came with certain commitments that had to be met, and the restructuring of the economy was an imperative for the Bank. Narasimha Rao and Manmohan Singh happened to be at the right place at the right time. The economic reforms of the 1990s that the Narasimha Rao government ushered in were the foundation on which the modern metropolis of New Delhi or the city I call New New Delhi was built. Although Rao's Great Leap Forward was dictated more by necessity than anything else, the fact was that once it was upon us there was no option but to go with the flow. Naturally, there were plenty of people who exploited the opportunities on offer for their own benefit. Creative corruption flourished.

The crippling nexus between the politician, the administration and the business class, became the pivot for aggrandizement without the necessary reconstitution of the laws that ruled enterprise. It seemed to be a godsend for the ruling class, which interpreted the laws to suit the moment; a general decline in morality followed, diminishing all that could have been positive with this 'change'. Leaders did not lead India out of the initial mess but instead reinforced the horrors with their silent, tacit participation and, therefore, approval. The disease stared to permeate life and living. Dilli was growing up, becoming an adult, a grihasthi.

With liberalization, albeit half-hearted, a new middle class, energetic and vibrant, infused with international middle-class aspirations, was beginning to make its intangible dreams into reality. Real estate boomed for the first time after New Delhi had been built. This time though, the controlled graciousness of the forties and fifties had given way to a robust flamboyance where new wealth and prosperity was blatantly visible. There was a shift in style and manner. Architecture symbolized fantasies and ambitions with the facades of mansions and bungalows imitating a 'Spanish hacienda', an 'English manor house', or a 'French chateau'. I have always wondered what life was like behind those closed doors. Were the inmates a trifle uncomfortable in their alien, adopted habitats? Gautam Bhatia, an eclectic architect, wrote a series of articles for *India Magazine* on 'Punjabi Chippendale' and 'Sindhi Baroque' that well described that period of real estate growth.

At around the same time, there was a rise in crass wealth, epitomized in the 'farmhouse-culture' that was taking root. I often wondered whether this reflected the latent desire of the owners of these 'farmhouses' to return to the comfort of Bharat every weekend, or were they imitating the retreat on Friday of Europeans to the 'country home'? Typically, these farmhouses would have long driveways that were invariably lined with alien species of trees like the silver oak, replacing the gulmohar, laburnum, kachnaar and varieties of champa. Each would have yards of manicured lawns bordered by flowerbeds, and these would be venues for elaborate, boozy, gossipy lunches in the winter sun. Naturally, these lunches would be 'catered'. Everything would be supplied by caterers, from the tented canopies under which tables would be laid to hired crockery, cutlery, glasses, and of course, a vast array of food—continental as it was called, Chinese and Mughlai. The 'salad bar' appeared on the scene and soon became as popular as the pasta counters that followed. Entertainment was taking on a different avatar. Wherever you went, whatever you ate, it looked and tasted the same, like canteen food in school; even the Indian cuisine no longer tasted authentic, infused as it was with oodles of garam masala.

When I got married in 1971 there was one well-established, wedding caterer—Greens. Of course, there were the traditional halwais who brought all their paraphernalia to the venue and cooked delicious, memorable feasts for the family and friends for days on end until the marriage. 'Chef' Babu was the master from Purani Dilli. His bhaturas, chicken korma and biryani have not been matched till date; his Anarkali kulfi has now become an unattainable mirage.

There was no wedding planner in our time. Friends and family did everything from the flower rangoli to mehndi to the accompanying song and dance. Today, turnkey weddings are the norm, boring, predictable and sterile, in a manner of speaking. Hired singers and dancers perform as all the rest watch. Participation is superficial. The personal touch has disappeared. The inherent mazaa has gone. Life is now orchestrated from the outside. Professional 'planners' will, for a fee, 'plan' weddings, bridal wardrobes, sing-songs, dinner parties, and all else. The movingly delicate traditions like mehndi and vatna have been structured and are impersonal society events.

÷

As the times changed, so did Delhi. A consequence of the open economy was Delhi being anointed as a metropolitan city. The burgeoning middle class reached out to devour all that was denied for decades under an earlier set of economic regulations, and thousands of migrants poured into the city in search of employment opportunities and better lifestyles.

Delhi was gradually assuming the title of India's

cultural and intellectual hub taking the baton from Bombay, drawing the traveller, explorer and visitor into her all-embracing self. She had become the media and publishing capital as well, attracting the best and brightest from overseas and from the other states of India. Ideas started to become a reality here. Seasons and activities melted seamlessly into one another making all twelve months of the year 'the season'. Music in Nehru Park; bands playing in the central park of Connaught Place; plays staged against the backdrop of the Purana Qila and within the proscenium arch of other cultural institutions; qawwali at Nizamuddin dargah; conferences, lectures, international trade fairs and music extravaganzas; grand polo tournaments; as well as events sponsored by the many embassies representing the 'world', like book fairs, great exhibitions and more, had the city saturated.

Gradually, a new generation of enterprising men and women, stepping out of the obvious professions of being lawyers, doctors, and members of the privileged fraternity of the IAS, and starting to opt for new opportunities in banking, in the hospitality sector, in journalism, film and television, compelled a vibrant tide of talent to flow into the city limits.

The Dilli of today is soulful, personal and confident in its multiple skins and has extended out in all directions, from its core and torso into the National Capital Region. Neighbouring Haryana showcased Gurgaon as the contemporary hub of commerce and new age businesses, as well as the residential bastion for a new generation. Gated colonies encompassed within their guarded fenced-in compounds offered all amenities from grocery shops with packaged foods to health clubs, swimming pools, to putting greens and gyms, and more. They rose out of the barren land to mark the new skyline. Brick, mortar and stone embellished with jaalis, pillared verandahs and cool courtyards had given way to high-rise concrete, glass and chrome. Personal trainers became the new daily fix replacing traditional masseurs who went from house to house carrying family gossip. Yoga was suddenly resurrected and became one of the new fads, and yoga mats became an essential product in fancy shops, as did whitening face cream. Women switched from wearing fabulous saris to strange ball gowns that made them look virtually 'dismembered' from their culture.

As the middle class became more upwardly mobile and style conscious, Fashion Week became a fixture on the city's cultural menu. Delhi was thus elevated to the position of the fashion capital of India, while Mumbai, particularly after her name change, slipped into a lowly second position.

And then, very recently, to top it all, came the Metro. Effective public transport is a great 'leveller' and destroys the pools of exclusivity that diminish a city. In Delhi, flyovers had linked far-flung areas that had been difficult to access via crowded four-lane roads and were, till recently, near forgotten, neglected, longing to be energized. The Metro changed all that. New eating places opened in local colony markets; boutiques sprouted; sleepy neglected parts of town became more spirited as the bazaars became diverse and attractive, selling all manner of specialties—from food to accessories and books and magazines from across the world, from beauty parlours, gyms and art galleries, to bathroom and kitchen stores.

Contradictions too, began to take root. A hitherto unknown animal called a Mall, strode on to the Delhi space demanding footfalls. It was, in comparison to neighbourhood bazaars, cold and impersonal, very compartmentalized but 'efficient', selling a new consumer ethos.

In the process, the Dilli of my youth was losing its many treasured and fragile cultural identities as we all fell into the rut of the oncoming mall, package and self-help culture.

Some of us missed the facilities we had once taken for granted. In an effort to cling on to my happiest moments, I kept up my close links with the man who made our chiks and chatais; the patwa, who restrung my necklaces and fixed broken bits of jewellery, utterly trustworthy professionals and experts because in those days, in my growing years, trust was a given; the cobbler who attached new soles to slippers and shoes that had become like a second skin; the darzi who would cut and stitch a sari blouse overnight because you needed it done fast; the dhobi whose jugaan came each week with our sheets white and spotless, smelling clean and crisp, unlike the limp rags that emerge from a washing machine, doused in bleach and sprayed with a chemical fragrance; the kalaiwallah who would visit

once a month to tin our thaalis; the fruit vendor who
knew my love for the sharifa—sitaphal of my Bombay
days—and would deliver the best of the season to the
door; the namkeenwallah from Gujarat with his array
of salty goodies; the carpet man from Kashmir who
washed our old rugs with love and care and would
bring a pot of honey for us every Diwali from the valley
before the snow set in; and others like the plumber, the
electrician, the carpenter, the painter, all 'old faithfuls',
eternally on call and dependable.

÷

The New Delhi of the mid-1900s, built by Edwin
Lutyens, Herbert Baker and their extended team of
architects and engineers, has gradually retreated into
its isolated, protective shell and became a well-tended
green island, the last breathing lung of this gargantuan
metro. Its residents too, have started to become more
and more insular, ruling from their carefully preserved
ivory towers, becoming increasingly disconnected from
a dynamic new India. That schism gets more and more
pronounced between the rulers and the ruled with each
passing moment.

÷

If I am asked to sum up my feelings about this New
New Delhi, I must admit that I cannot quite make up
my mind, which is as it should be for any city that looks
to cement its position among the mega cities of the
twenty-first century.

Today, in the first quarter of the twenty-first century, visible changes are taking place all the time in Dilli, some delightful, some painful. This new avatar is active, energized and raring to experience and experiment with all that comes its way. Competitive and increasingly volatile in its expression and style, this new Dilli has become a real city. There is a buzz here like never before. As I grow older, it is this new liveliness that makes me feel young and intellectually agile. It also makes me feel like an alien, exploring the space again, looking for missed treasures and new ideas, engineering within my person, a new excitement.

Some of the newness agitates the mind and soul. When I am asked to go to dinner for a 'fine food' meal in a mall, I shudder with unease. For me, malls serve fast food to shoppers on the trot. In a similar genre, hotels, under the banner of five-stars, have proliferated, beckoning local residents to partake in eating international cuisine in badly lit restaurants, where the food is usually over-priced, fake and unappetizing. But, the wonderful change now is the sprouting of delightful restaurants in the many bazaars of town, like anywhere else in the world, that serve up creative, good meals at reasonable prices. Delhi has matured into a foodie's city again. It is, in fact, the food capital of India. Kwality, with its outstanding brain masala; Kake da Hotel, the quintessential city dhaba; and many other specialty eating-places continue to thrive, alongside the more recent Smokehouse Deli, Diva, Tres and Rara Avis, to name a few.

There are some wonderful things that can only happen in Dilli. I recall a dinner hosted by Momin Latif many years ago where he bundled us all into a bus and took us to the Old City to the iconic restaurant, Karim's, where he had set up a spectacularly stylish table, complete with a white damask tablecloth, candelabra, silver cutlery, crystal glasses, china plates and large comfortable serviettes. We sat down to a dinner of kebabs and raan, biryani and bheja. Utterly delicious, utterly special, etched forever in my mind. I doubt that such a traditional feast could be served in such a stylish way anywhere else in the world, particularly in a setting as distinctive as that alley in the old city.

+

120

In the past, family biographies and social histories were passed down through the generations by grandmothers and widowed aunts who recalled all the delicious details of relationships and intrigue, of conversations and expeditions, of the division of properties, of greed and dishonour. Those gently nuanced, personal family stories were narrated through word of mouth, as were our ancient philosophies, and remained alive, embellished periodically by new storytellers to make for a better narrative. They were our 'bhandaars' or camphor chests of bits and pieces of information, however ordinary and seemingly inconsequential, that came together as a many-layered tapestry of a tangible and shared social legacy, heritage and DNA. They were our bedtime stories, in a manner of speaking.

Today, toddlers are growing up without the magical bedtime story. There are no old-world family retainers who can rattle off episodes of the *Mahabharata* with the expert ease of a professional storyteller. Kids are condemned to some rather sloppy and shoddy, stilted and unimpressive television shows before lights out. As a grandmother, I impatiently look forward to passing on the many encounters and experiences of my life to another generation, as a counterpoint to the all-consuming, cold and impersonal internet of their present and future. Both have a place. The best of both should be exploited and shared.

EPILOGUE

When I was in my late thirties, my mother was diagnosed with cancer and fifteen months later, having decided not to fight the ghastly disease, passed on at the age of sixty in April 1987. She had lived a very complete and fulsome life with my father, sharing virtually every moment with him, living and working together. He was prime in her life, all of us followed. He could not deal with her death, collapsed emotionally, pushed himself to go to work each morning, hating every moment of it and followed her to the grave, for no reason apart from being unable to mend a severely shredded heart. He died in August of the same year at the age of sixty-four. I was orphaned and emotionally maimed. Having been raised in a family where privacy was guarded and respected, I disappeared within my own person with my pain. Next morning, Tejbir—who loved both my parents as much as I did—and I, went off to work, 'operating' with a false veneer of being normal. The September issue of the magazine had to be posted on 31 August and meeting that deadline was our first priority. It is what my parents would have expected of us and we were not about to let them down.

Seminar had been left to Tejbir and I. We were privileged to inherit their intangible and precious legacy, the third child they had nurtured with great care and fortitude. I recall some unpleasant whispers about how this 'institution' would probably disappear in Mala's hands; how Mala was wonderful and amusing but would she be able to pull off a forum for the intelligentsia month after month; how Mala is more of an 'influential society hostess' than someone who is known for her journalistic skills, and so on. All this despite the fact that I had been responsible for starting, with Ashok Advani, India's first business magazine and the first magazine of India's larger culture. Having heard one particular academic say this to his colleague, both friends of my father, I was determined to show them the paces of another generation. For us, that 'inheritance' has been the anchor for our incredible and tumultuous life, the foundation that has connected us with a new generation of professionals across all disciplines. In the evening, like my parents before me, Tejbir and I invite a wide range of wonderful people to our home to share a meal and lively conversation. Our home, too, is an open house like my parents' home was at Kautilya Marg.

Our office is in the same space overlooking Connaught Place. There has been no break in the culture of the office. As I walk from the parking lot of F Block to the staircase that leads to our office, the woman selling bananas greets me, the magazine vendor hands me

123

something to read, the man who polishes shoes asks whether I have brought a bag of shoes for a good shine, and then, feeling good about being in my familiar surroundings, I enter my cocoon. It has bright coloured walls, comfortable chairs that belong to the design idiom of the fifties, bookshelves, a dining table, endless paintings, photographs, posters and maps, frayed carpets on the floor, a home away from home. A tiffin carrier from the days of yore brings lunch from home. Friends and contributors drop by, ideas are bounced around, arguments ensue, young writers and academics energize and excite my mind and the really taaza khabar, word-of-mouth information of what is happening behind the scenes, is shared with abandon . . . What would life be without a daily dose of fresh 'gossip' over the best-brewed coffee in town? That great Indian oral tradition keeps us connected and perpetually engaged.

Every so often, Jaisal drops by for his favourite mutton kathi roll from Nizam's. Sandip Dikshit comes by for egg sandwiches. Mahesh Rangarajan will bring his tiffin and eat with us. Ananya and Basharat will spend a long afternoon discussing Kashmir, or Ananya's latest book, *Righteous Republic*. The Maharaja of Kapurthala will come to get his subscription renewed and not want to disturb us till he is spotted and brought in to have a coffee with us. T.N. Ninan and I will argue vociferously over lunch, and so it goes on. The list is infinite. The postman greets me each morning and has a brief chat. The table I sit at is a hand-me-down from Dr Karan Singh when he re-did his library sometime in

124

the seventies. Tejbir and our colleague, Harsh Sethi, sit
at desks that my parents used in the *Crossroads* days in
Bombay. We hang on to the tangibles of an intangible
past. We move on with the memories protecting us,
comfortable in our skin. As the city moves into a newer
avatar, and as we carefully walk the obstacle course to
avoid hurting ourselves with sharp edged change, one
realizes how fortunate my generation is to witness yet
another phase of Dilli, this city of my heart.

ACKNOWLEDGEMENTS

Being a hesitant 'writer', reticent about putting it all down in words, I was happily surprised and honoured when David Davidar suggested I write this short biography of a city I have come to love. This book is a personal description of the Delhi I know and my life within it. Thank you, David, for signing me on and for your skilful and deft interventions.

I was in bed, unable to walk having broken both my legs, when I signed off on the contract and thought I would fill the long hours of those three months writing this 'biography'. Strangely, I could get no work done at all on the manuscript, not even put random ideas and words down on paper. The brain ceased to function as I wallowed in constant dull pain, complete constriction of movement, but with huge amounts of friendship, much conversation around me, delicious food and lots of laughter, as friends and acquaintances filled the many hours of day and night that could well have been painfully long and lonely. Delhi had embraced me in my most difficult moment.

I started writing as soon as I could walk again. If I

have been emotional, it is because I realized, as I recovered from a disabling accident, that Dilli and those who people it have given my life meaning and sustenance over fifty wonderful years. I am grateful to my extended family, my own and that of Tejbir's, to our very special, old and more recent friends, and a stream of delightful acquaintances who have all come together and created an extraordinary and unusual tapestry that is our life in Delhi. I thank them for their affection and patience.

Aruna Ghose, who I have known from my Bombay days when we were both little girls, and who worked with me years later on the *India Magazine*, was, ironically, my editor on this book. Many thanks, Aruna, for bearing with all my quirky responses and more. The cover of this book comes from the vibrant imagination of Premola Ghose who has, over the years, painted whimsical and some iconic images that define this layered city and its unmatched imprints. Thank you, Premola. Kiran Anand, a dear friend of recent years, and Anabel Loyd, an old friend, both read through the first draft, and calmed my hyper nervous tension! Thank you both for sparing the time and for giving me your inputs. Simar and Aienla, thank you both for being the best in the business, silently pushing me on, helping me along the way. My gratitude to Bena for putting the many pieces together with such flair.

Tejbir and Jaisal, my staunchest critics but also my unfailing support system, and Anjali, always there for me, have made much of my carefree and liberated life possible. Words are no measure for what I owe them for their love, patience, friendship and camaraderie. I have dedicated this personal memoir of Delhi to Amrit and Sujan, my grandchildren and the joy of my life, who will hopefully live their lives to the fullest in this ancient, modern metropolis.

www.ingramcontent.com/pod-product-compliance
Lightning Source LLC
Chambersburg PA
CBHW010236100426
42812CB00032B/3347/J